IN ACCOUNT WITH
Lansky Bros. Men's Shop
and Formal Rentals
TELEPHONE
MEMPHIS, TENN.
THE FIRST NATIONAL BANK
PAY TO THE ORDER OF
DOLLARS
No. E 2018
540 BROADWAY · NEW YORK 12, N.Y.
No 5135
STATEMENT
BALTIMORE 1, MD.
AETNA SHIRT CO.
MAKERS OF
High Grade Shirts
TERMS
Persona Labels
ITEM
MEMPHIS, TENN.
THE FIRST NATIONAL BANK
DOLLARS
PAY TO THE ORDER OF

To: Gary
May we all have the style of Elvis!
Sincerely,
Hal J. Lansky

LANSKY BROTHERS
CLOTHIER TO THE KING

It was a pleasure to meet you! However don't step on our Blue Suede Shoes!

Hal J. Lansky

4-28-16

LANSKY BROTHERS
CLOTHIER TO THE KING

SINCE 1946

FOREWORD BY BERNARD J. LANSKY

BECKON BOOKS

Lansky Bros
MEN'S SHOP
on famous Beale Street

GOOSE TATUM
MARQUES HAYNES
SUN. 15 ELLIS AUD.

126 Formal Wear For Rent

"Just Around

CLOTHING · LUGGAGE

Quick CONFIDENTIAL LOANS

to LOAN

124

from

CLOTHING · LUGGAGE

TABLE OF CONTENTS

FOREWORD 12

PART ONE: BEALE STREET BEGINNINGS 18

PART TWO: THE KING'S NEW CLOTHES 38

PART THREE: THE LANSKY LEGACY 102

WWW.LANSKYBROS.COM

OPPOSITE | Signs of the Times
*A view of the famous Lansky Brothers sign on Beale Street, circa 1950s.
Over the years, the store became a historical landmark in downtown Memphis.*

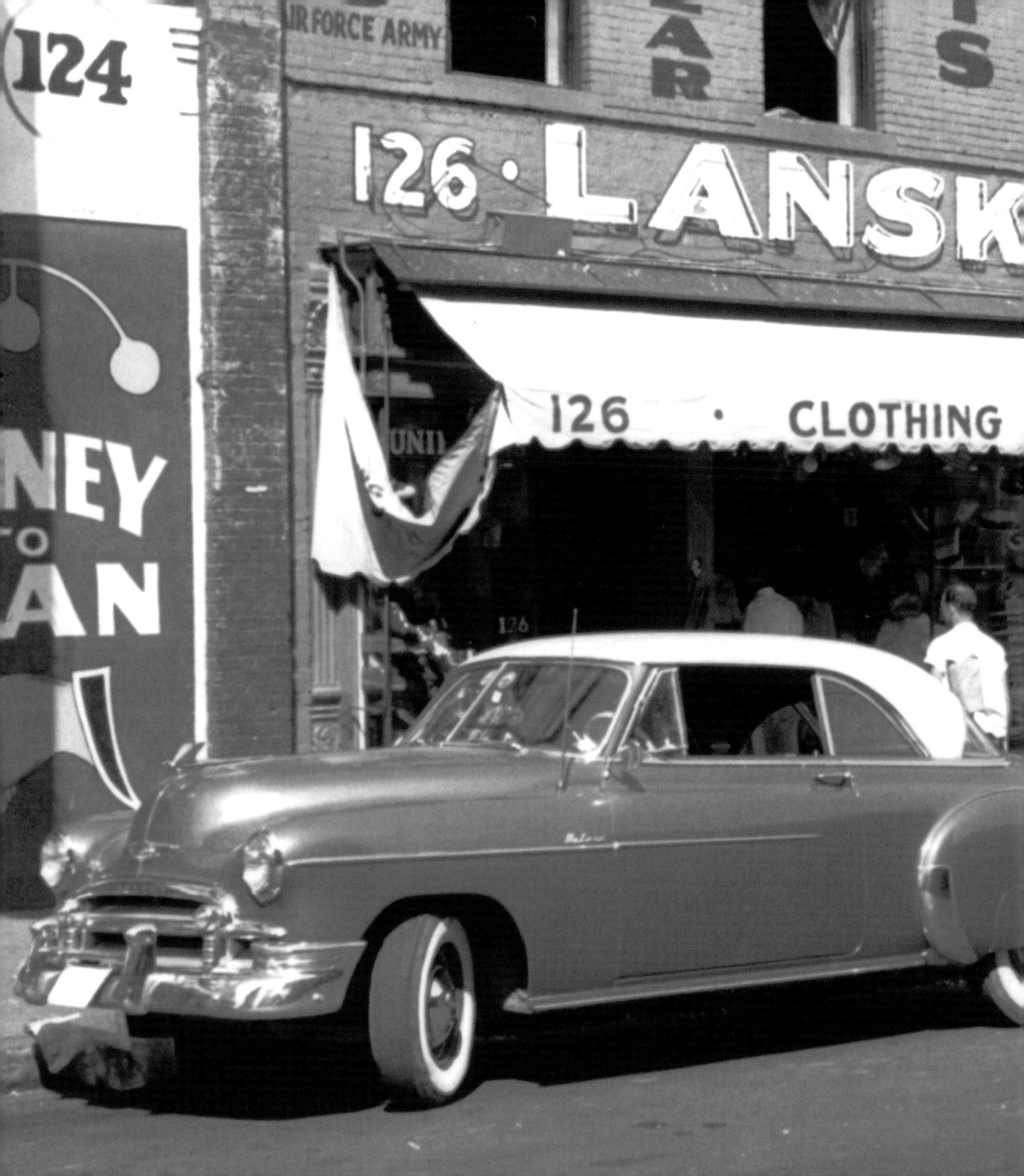
124
AIR FORCE ARMY
126 · LANSK
126 · CLOTHING
NEY
O
AN
126

BROS. 126
MISSISSIPPI RIVER
Goldcrest
51
BEER
LUGGAGE • JEWELRY • 126

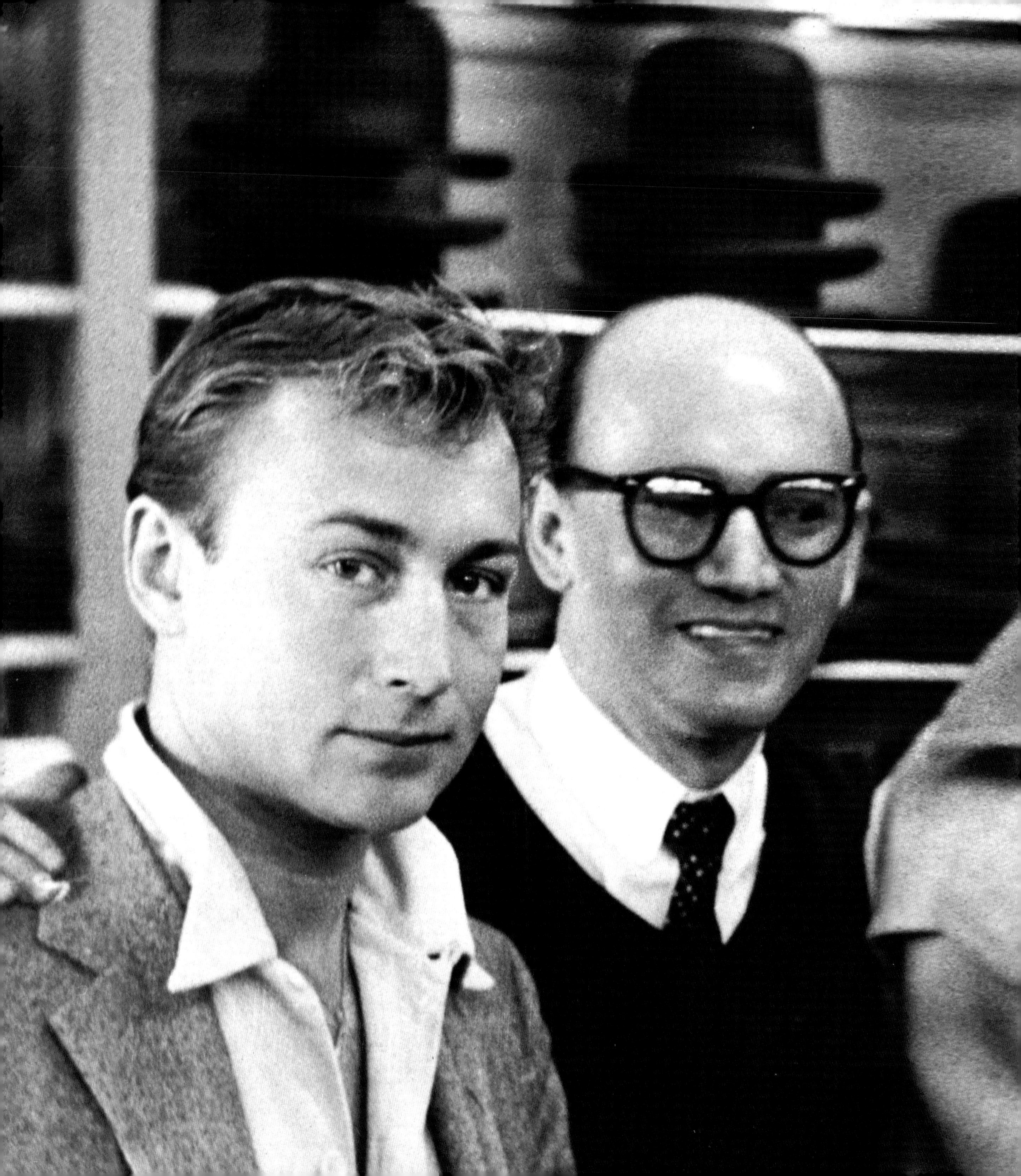

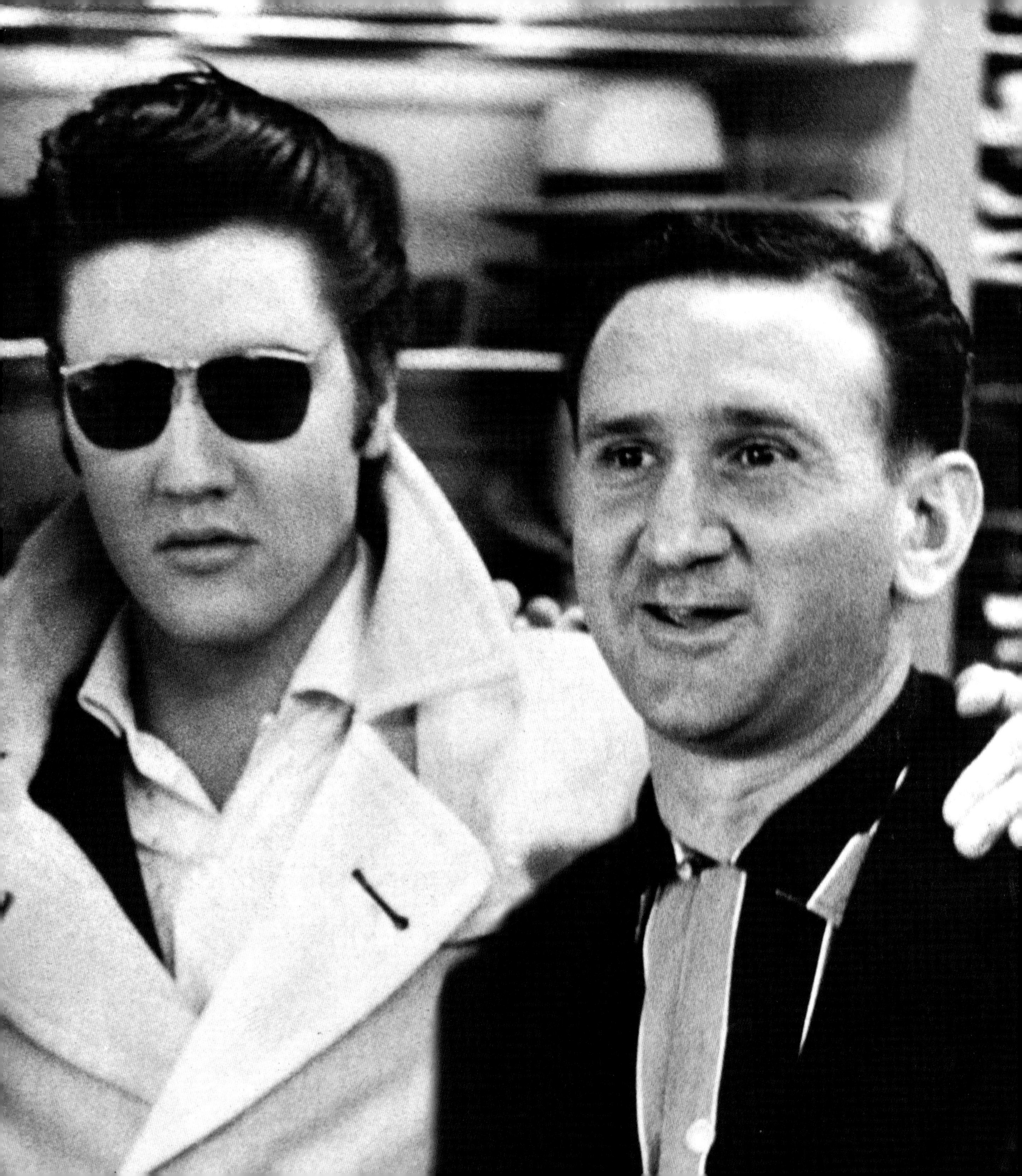

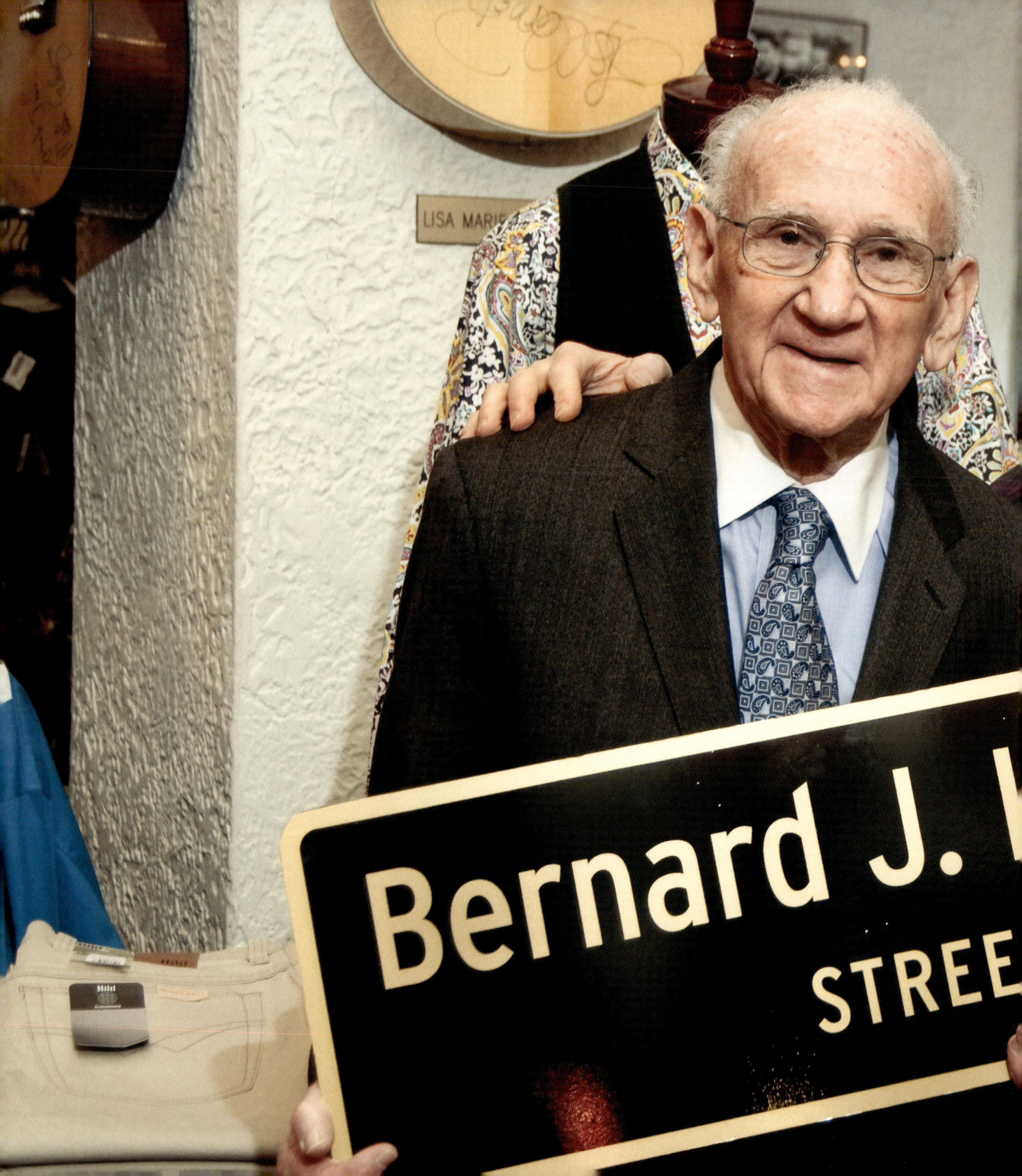
LISA MARIE
Bernard J. L
STREE

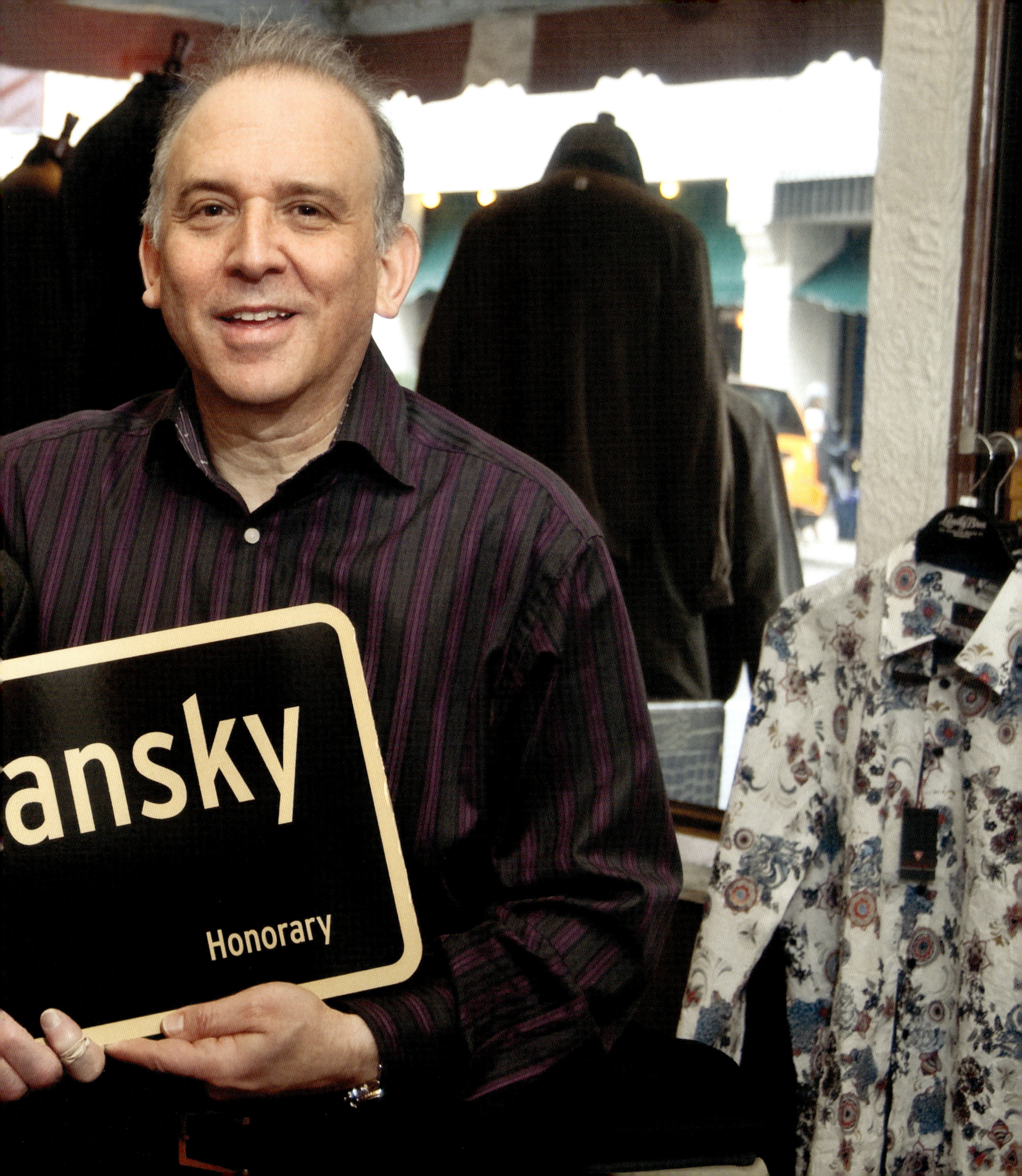
ansky
Honorary

ELVIS FASHION
Elvis Fashion Books
Autographed by
Bernard Lansky
"Clothier to the King"
SINGER

Foreword

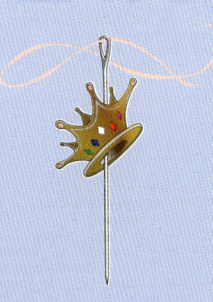

It's hard to imagine that more than six decades have passed since we opened a small army surplus shop on an unknown street named Beale. My siblings and I started with very limited knowledge of how to run a business. The only piece of advice came from our father, who opened the door for me on my eighteenth birthday and said, "Son, here's the world—now go and get it." This instilled in me a curiosity and drive to keep hustling and changing with the times.

Lansky Brothers was born on a street that had a reputation for having down-south juke joints and thriving pawn shops; by opening a clothing store there, we were ahead of our time. With each decade, we've continued to stay ahead of the trends. In the fifties, we dressed men in pink and black, a color combination that was unheard of at the time. We brought to Memphis the mod fashions from London's Carnaby Street during the sixties.

OPPOSITE | Memphis Ties
Bernard Lansky has clothed dozens of musicians, actors, and athletes since 1946.

RIGHT | All in the Family
Hal, Julie, and Bernard Lansky accept an Uptown/Downtown Award in July 2008 from New York trade publication MR *magazine, which recognized Lansky's innovation and influence on fashion around the world.*

And we're still proud to say that in the seventies, we sold more men's stack heel shoes than any other store in the country! The eighties brought new adventures as we filled a much-needed niche in the Mid-South for Big and Tall men's clothing. And today, we sit comfortably nestled into the lobby of the famous Peabody hotel with four unique stores that cater to men and women of all ages.

I am very fortunate to have a family business that now incorporates three generations. I've watched my son Hal grow up in the retail business, and together, we have passed along the Lansky Brothers tradition of style and customer service to his daughter—and my granddaughter—Julie. As I reflect on the past that we have built together, I am also awed by what Beale Street has become internationally. I never could have imagined being a part of such a storied history, or being such an influence on one of the most famous entertainers of all time. Our popularity was carved from dressing one man who became famous, but our legacy has been crafted from more than sixty years of customer service to people from around the world.

We cherish each person who has ever walked through our doors. Thank you for being a part of our storied past—and our exciting future!

Bernard J. Lansky
Bernard J. Lansky
January 2010

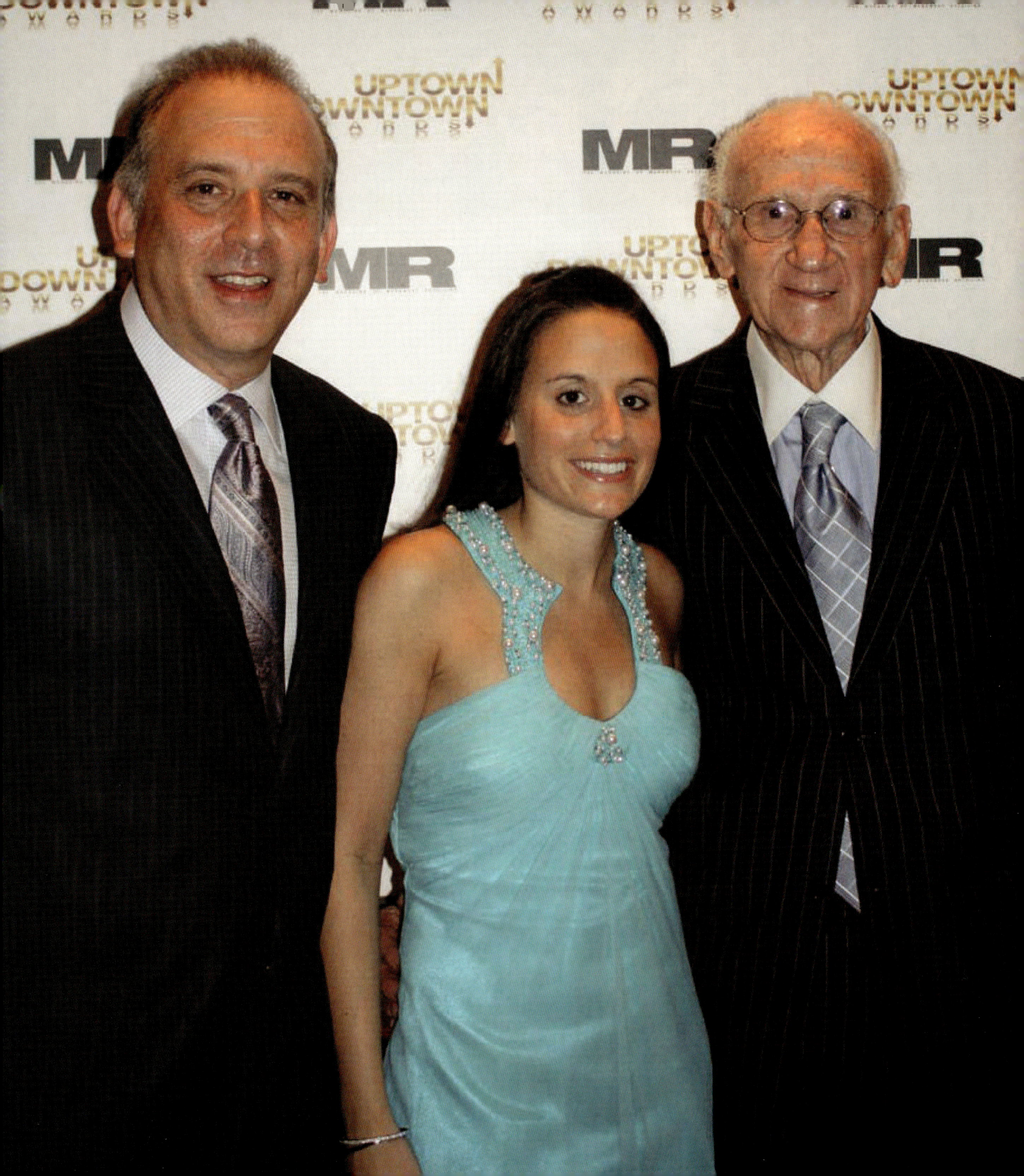

UPTOWN
MIR

From left to right: Bernard, Guy, and Mildred Lansky stand outside the original Lansky Brothers army surplus store in the late 1940s, looking out at Beale Street. For a time, the brothers also ran a uniform business, as evidenced by the truck pictured in the foreground. The uniform business only lasted for a short time; when the surplus clothing ran out by the early 1950s, they decided to focus on high-fashion men's clothing.

GGAGE
WELRY
BROS. 126
MISSISSIPPI
LUGGAGE
WATCH REPAIRS
LANSKY BROS.
UNIFORM CO.
126 BEALE
5-5401
244 N. MAIN
37-0116
1670 KANSAS
35-5980
Lettered
UNIFORMS
for
Distinction

18   LANSKY BROTHERS: *CLOTHIER TO THE KING*

Part One

BEALE STREET BEGINNINGS

1946–1952

EVEN BEFORE ELVIS PRESLEY TOOK THE WORLD by storm with his swiveling hips and soulful hits, Lansky Brothers was making its own mark. Nestled among the bars, blues clubs, and brothels on historically black Beale Street in Memphis, the Lansky Brothers men's clothing store sold ultra-hip "cat clothes" in the 1940s and 50s to the fashion savvy young people and black musicians who performed nearby.

The offerings at Lansky contrasted starkly to the clean-cut and traditional styles popular with midcentury Americans. Lansky Brothers featured colorful window displays with bright colors and flashy designs that were intended to pop onstage. This, of course, was precisely what would catch the attention of a young Elvis Presley in 1952. Yet the store that would become "Clothier to the King" got an unassuming start.

LEFT | **Surplus Style**
An early photo of the Lansky Brothers army surplus store. Like many retailers in the area after the war, the brothers sold cast-offs from the local army depot—along with an assortment of paint, luggage, and jewelry.

ABOVE | Fifties Fashion
Samuel Lewis Lansky, Bernard's father, with a selection of cabana sets, circa 1950. Cabana sets—popular men's leisure wear in the 1950s—were often lined with terry cloth and featured button-down, loose-fitting shirts and elastic-waist shorts.

In 1946, Russian immigrant Samuel Lewis Lansky bought a secondhand store for $125 at 126 Beale Street, hoping to ensure that his sons—who had just returned from stints in the army—would have secure futures with steady jobs. Samuel Lansky was a hard worker and a retail veteran. After arriving from Grodno, Russia, in 1910, he had opened a grocery store on Kansas Street, where his nine children worked. His son Bernard Lansky remembers: "Early on, my daddy gave me the best advice in the world. He took me over to a window, pointed outside, and said, 'Here's the world, son; now go out and get it.' Nothing was ever handed to me, and working hard was just part of life."

The new store, which sold used ladies' clothing, came with a bit of notoriety: The previous owner had been murdered inside. The Lanskys, however, were undaunted. Samuel Lansky handed over the keys to his sons, and they quickly changed up the hand-me-down inventory. "I took one look around and said, 'It ain't me,'" Bernard remembers of the secondhand ladies' merchandise. The brothers literally tossed everything on the street and watched as people grabbed the stock and ran.

Unfortunately, there wasn't much merchandise available to replace it. The only goods around after the war were army surplus. And with the Great Depression and World War II being a recent memory, people didn't want to spend a lot of money on clothes. The brothers went to the army depot and bought up boxes and boxes of military clothing. They sold caps for fifty cents and fatigue shirts or pants for $1.95.

The problem was, "practically everybody in town was selling the same ol' stuff," says Bernard. No one in Memphis was

ABOVE | Banking on Success
An early Lansky Brother's bankbook from the Commercial Industrial Bank, with entries dated from December 24, 1946, to June 30, 1947.

20 LANSKY BROTHERS: *CLOTHIER TO THE KING*

selling high fashion merchandise. So when the army surplus market dried up around 1950, Bernard and Guy began offering stylish men's clothing. "I started high fashion for the ethnic people," Bernard says. "They needed clothing to wear for their bands, church gospel groups, and concerts."

The venture was a word-of-mouth success. Beale Street in the 1950s was brimming with theaters and clubs, and many people liked to walk up and down the street. Bernard started "dressin' windows," luring the area's great musicians into Lansky Brothers to select bolts of fabric for their suits. There, they could choose from high-fashion mohairs, silks, wools, and sharkskins—all patterned in outlandish hues from purple to chartreuse to gold.

LEFT | Family Matters
Described in a press release as "the Brooks Brothers of the Mid-South," the Lansky brothers—seen wearing double-breasted suits at Bernard's wedding in 1948—were always fashion forward. Pictured from left to right are: Irvin, Guy, Bernard, Frank, Jack, and Alvin.

The store's tailors did impressive work, logging long hours cutting, making, and trimming. Young people often dropped by on Monday and requested their clothing by Saturday night. Many of Lansky's clients were bands, choirs, or other groups of entertainers who wanted something "a little different" for their performances; no one wanted to look alike. They chose way-out fashions such as Hi-Boy collar shirts, pants without back pockets, and fabric in every color of the rainbow.

"We carried nothing but the finest," says Bernard. "That's what the kids of the late forties, early fifties wanted. And we gave it to them."

BEALE STREET BEGINNINGS

By the early 1950s, the store was focused on high fashion, offering far-out clothes in the latest styles, including California peggers, roomy pants that tapered to the cuff; Ivy League–style clothing such as single-breasted blazers with natural shoulders and narrow lapels; and Levi's jeans, made popular by Hollywood actors such as James Dean and Marlon Brando.

ABOVE | **The Memphis Mile**

For years, Beale Street at night was as lively as during the day. Clubs and theaters crowded the nearly two-mile-long strip, which brimmed with music from famous jazz and blues artists such as B. B. King, Louis Armstrong, and Muddy Waters.

"We had *so many people* comin' in that we didn't have store hours—we were busy from *sunup to sundown*."

—Bernard Lansky

BEALE STREET BEGINNINGS 23

ABOVE AND RIGHT | A Cut Above
To cater to the musicians and hipsters on historically black Beale Street, Lansky Brothers carried cutting-edge styles that were distinct from the wares offered by its more conservative competitors.

BELOW | Lansky's Calling Card
A 1950s business card bearing the motto: "The shop that sets the pace in styles for men's wear."

RIGHT | From Panamas to Porkpies
Lansky Brothers carried a wide variety of classic, 1950s Panama hats, including those made by "Adam Hat," a popular brand in the 1940s and 50s.

24 LANSKY BROTHERS: *CLOTHIER TO THE KING*

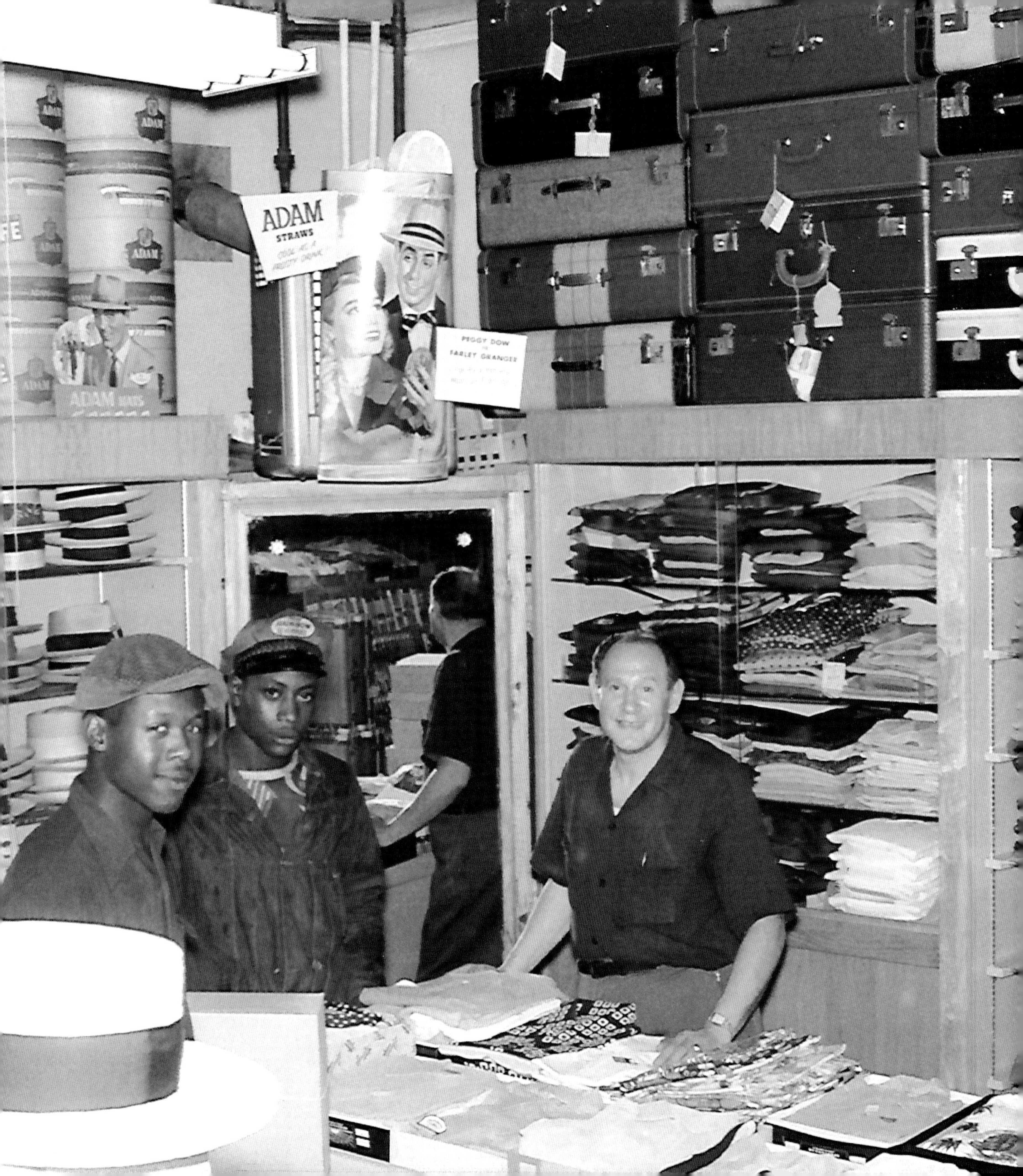
ADAM
STRAWS
PEGGY DOW
FARLEY GRANGER
ADAM HATS

Lansky Bros.

Cut a crazy caper with
The Hipster
A snake of a jacket – detachable hood. Water repellent poplin with warm quilted lining. Dog leash closings. Natural only...
Number 11 . . . $19.95

Wrap it up in the
Gone Rag
Exclusive LANSKY for stiffin' 'n jivin' . . . knit sleeves and collar with imported Heeksuede body. Blue/white, Tan/white, Brown/white . . . .
Number 12 . . . $19.95
Number 13 . . . as above with doeskin body $24.95

Tempt the dollies in
Drag Strip
Heavy wide-wale corduroy jacket in flashy red and black, with zipper front . . . .
Number 8 . . . $15.95

Get your kicks in
Super Cool
the shirt that comes two ways – either with neat mandarin collar or a wide spread collar. White, blue, grey. Extra small, small, medium large, large $4.95
Number 9 . . . mandarin collar $4.95
Number 10 . . wide spread collar 4.95

It's CRAZY man-CRAZY!
The Rock 'n Roll
Pat Boone says this jacket is something else! Of 100% all wool with a ribbed knit waistband. Black, Red, Powder Blue, Beige.
Number 1 . . . with sleeves $12.95
Number 2 . . . sleeveless   7.95
Number 3 . . the printed leather cap in a go-it-all color selection . . . 1.99

Get with it, mate-wear
Date Bait
The fanciest sport shirt in town! A jazzy blend of rayon/cotton/silk with a corduroy vest effect and pocket trim. Detailed with a sheer insert glittering with gold threads!
Number 4 . . . $4.95

Right: This ad from the 1950s reflected the styles and tastes of the store's young clientele, including a "Rock 'n' Roll" style jacket that singer Pat Boone called "something else!"

FASHION FORWARD

Early 1950s

When the army surplus business evaporated in the early 1950s, Bernard Lansky and his brother Guy began making trips to New York and California to find new and interesting clothes to offer the young people and entertainers on Beale Street. They returned with clothing that was unlike anything most of Memphis had ever seen.

Instead of the cardigan sweaters, dark flannel suits, and penny loafers that were being peddled in Hollywood and popular culture, Lansky Brothers offered mandarin-collared shirts, pegged pants, and clothing in what Bernard Lansky describes as "Life Savers colors"—reds, pinks, blues, yellows, and purples. The store also sold "booty tight" two-toned pants with no back pockets and inverted pleats, cut to show off the wearer's backside. The clothes and textures were intended to be flashy enough to stand out onstage or on the black-and-white TVs of the time—and they were.

Entertainers weren't the store's only customers. "In those days, Memphis had a lot of pimps, gamblers," Bernard recalls. "We had high fashion in the window. I'd do tailor-made mohair, silk, and wool. Flare leg. Twenty-six-inch knee, fourteen-inch bottom drape. Then I made thinner legs."

At first, the other merchants on Beale and nearby Main Street raised their eyebrows. "People thought we were crazy," Bernard chuckles. "They couldn't understand. They didn't think we would make it." That changed as more and more musicians came to buy their clothes from Lansky Brothers. "We sure fooled them," Bernard continues. "We didn't even have store hours—we were busy from sunup to sundown." Soon, Lansky was selling to the likes of B. B. King, Johnny Cash, Roy Orbison, Jerry Lee Lewis . . . and a poor, gangly teenager who was about to become the King of Rock 'n' Roll.

Above: Over the years, many family members worked in the store, including (left) Joyce Lansky, Bernard's wife, and Mildred Lansky, Bernard's sister.

Below: Like the merchandise itself, Lansky's window displays were eye-catching. Lansky Brothers had its own tailor shop, which allowed the store to take orders as late as Monday for the Friday night shows that took place on Beale Street.

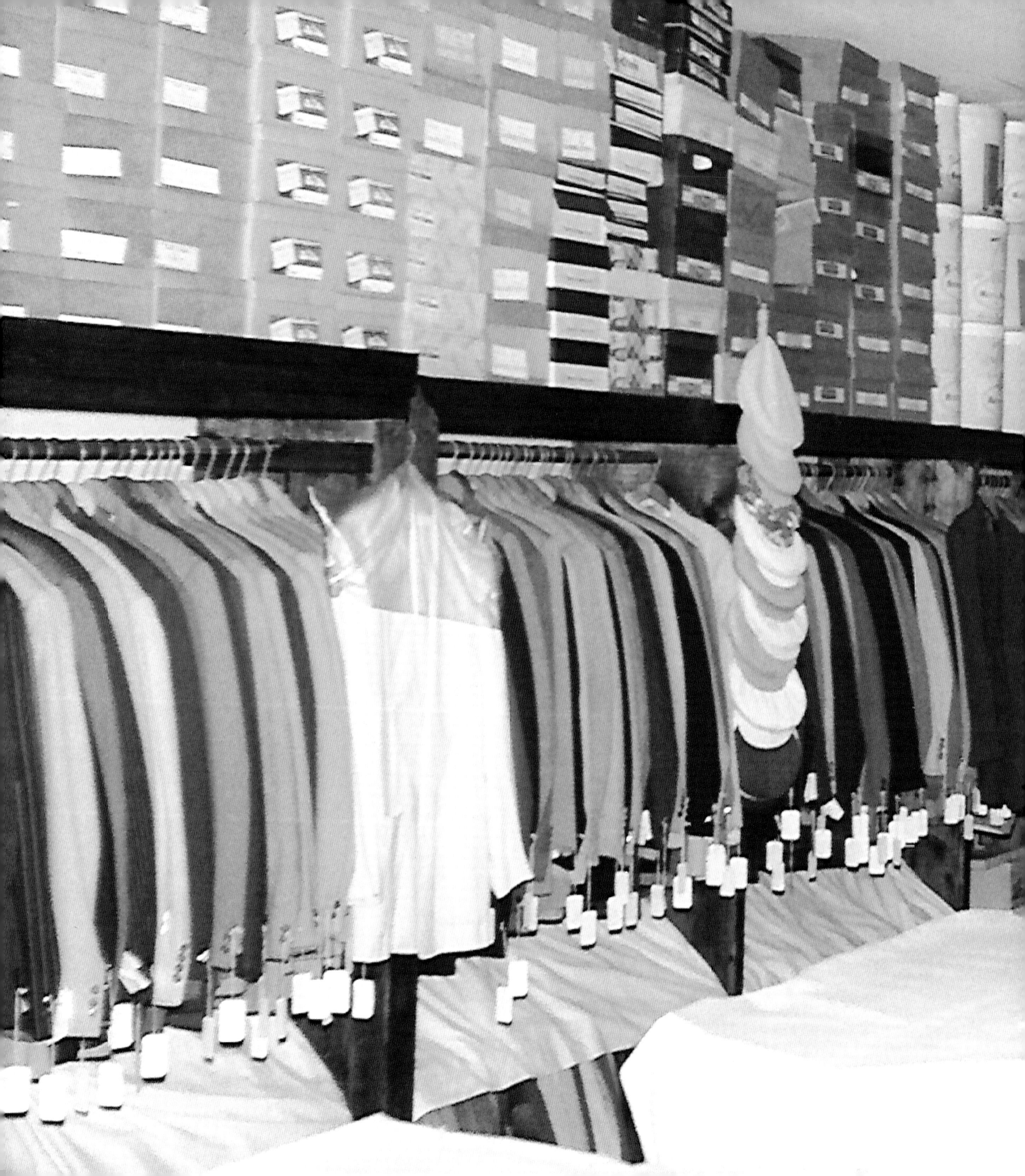

Lansky Brothers was one of the first stores on Beale Street to have air conditioning, a big draw for shoppers during the South's hot and humid summer months. Despite such advances, the ventilation systems of the 1950s and 1960s were primitive, requiring the Lanskys to cover their merchandise at night with sheets to protect it from the thick dust.

RIGHT AND OPPOSITE |

Hats off to Style

Until the 1950s, men traditionally wore a variety of hats, including fedoras, Panamas, porkpies, and newsboy caps, as seen on the customers here. The topcoats and shiny double-breasted vests, worn by entertainers preparing for a Saturday night on famous Beale, far right, were classic Lansky styles.

RIGHT | **Belts and Basics**

Skinny belts—and ties—were all the rage in the 1950s. Lansky Brothers sold hundreds of these "initials belts" for $1.50 each. Customers often wore them with peg-leg trousers.

"Our stuff was cutting-edge. We had the shirts with the balloon sleeves and two-tone pants with inverted pleats and no pockets in the back, so you could show off your booty when you were onstage."
—Bernard Lansky

30   LANSKY BROTHERS: *CLOTHIER TO THE KING*

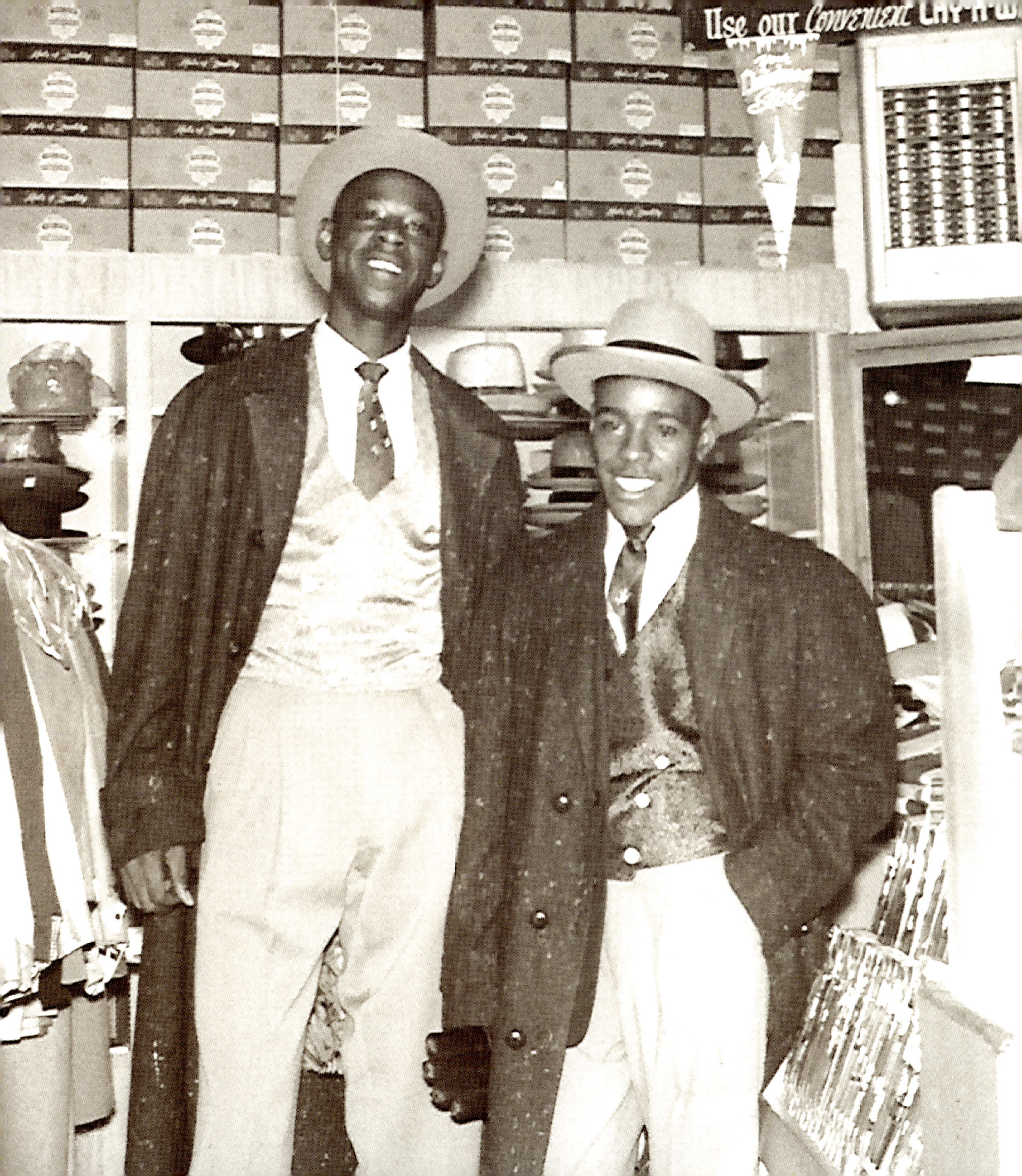
Use our Convenient

Lansky employees stand in front of the bronze W. C. Handy statue in the park named after the famous blues musician.

SINGING THE MEMPHIS BLUES

Beale Street

While Bernard Lansky was initially mocked for establishing a high-fashion store on Beale Street, he quickly proved his wisdom and foresight in doing so. The street, which extends nearly two miles through downtown Memphis, also claims a significant part of music history.

Beale Street was formed in the mid-1800s, but it wasn't until 1909, when famed blues composer W. C. Handy and his band came to town, that the area began to develop its reputation for music. That year, Handy was commissioned to write a campaign tune for aspiring Memphis mayoral candidate Edward Hull "Boss" Crump, who wanted to gain the black vote. Crump won, and the song became so popular that Handy rewrote the tune and renamed it "The Memphis Blues."

Handy was a prolific composer, writing many American classics during this period, including "The St. Louis Blues" and "Beale Street Blues." In the years that followed, other blues and jazz legends such as B. B. King, Memphis Minnie, Louis Armstrong, and Muddy Waters flocked to Beale Street. Under their influence, the term "The Memphis Blues" soon evolved from a song title to a bona fide music style. Memphis became known as the "Home of the Blues," with its blues bars, bands, and clubs buzzing with music through the night. And it was to this vibrant cultural strip that Elvis Presley was drawn, mesmerized by the heart and soul of the black musicians.

Above: W. C. Handy was a prolific blues musician and songwriter who helped to take the genre mainstream. Inspired by the black spirituals of the South, he composed such famous songs as "Beale Street Blues," "The Memphis Blues," and "The St. Louis Blues."

Below: The original sheet music to the song "The Memphis Blues."

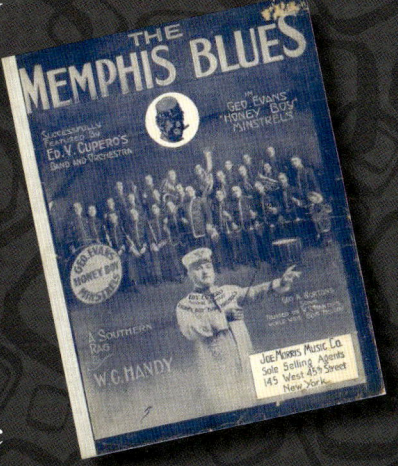

BEALE STREET BEGINNINGS

34 LANSKY BROTHERS: *CLOTHIER TO THE KING*

LEFT AND BELOW | The Best Service—and Style

Ever the salesman, Bernard Lansky worked around the clock to make sure his customers got "only the best." Pictured are some of Lansky's early clients picking up their boxing jackets, including the 1958 Tri-State Boxing Champion, left, and Willie Herenton, the 1959 Tri-State Boxing Champion who would later become mayor of Memphis, bottom left.

OPPOSITE | Cornering the Market

When Bernard and Guy Lansky opened Lansky Brothers, customers were cost-conscious, still reeling from the Great Depression and rationing of goods that took place during World War II. To lure frugal shoppers, the Lanskys emphasized value, saying that the store was "just around the corner from high prices."

"We used to have Life Savers colors: reds, pinks, blues, yellows, purples. We had it all."
—Bernard Lansky

BEALE STREET BEGINNINGS 35

Bernard often arrived at Lansky Brothers early in the morning, having done a day's business before his employees even clocked in. After opening the store, he liked to greet passersby on the sidewalk—the best position in which to lure would-be customers off the street and into the store.

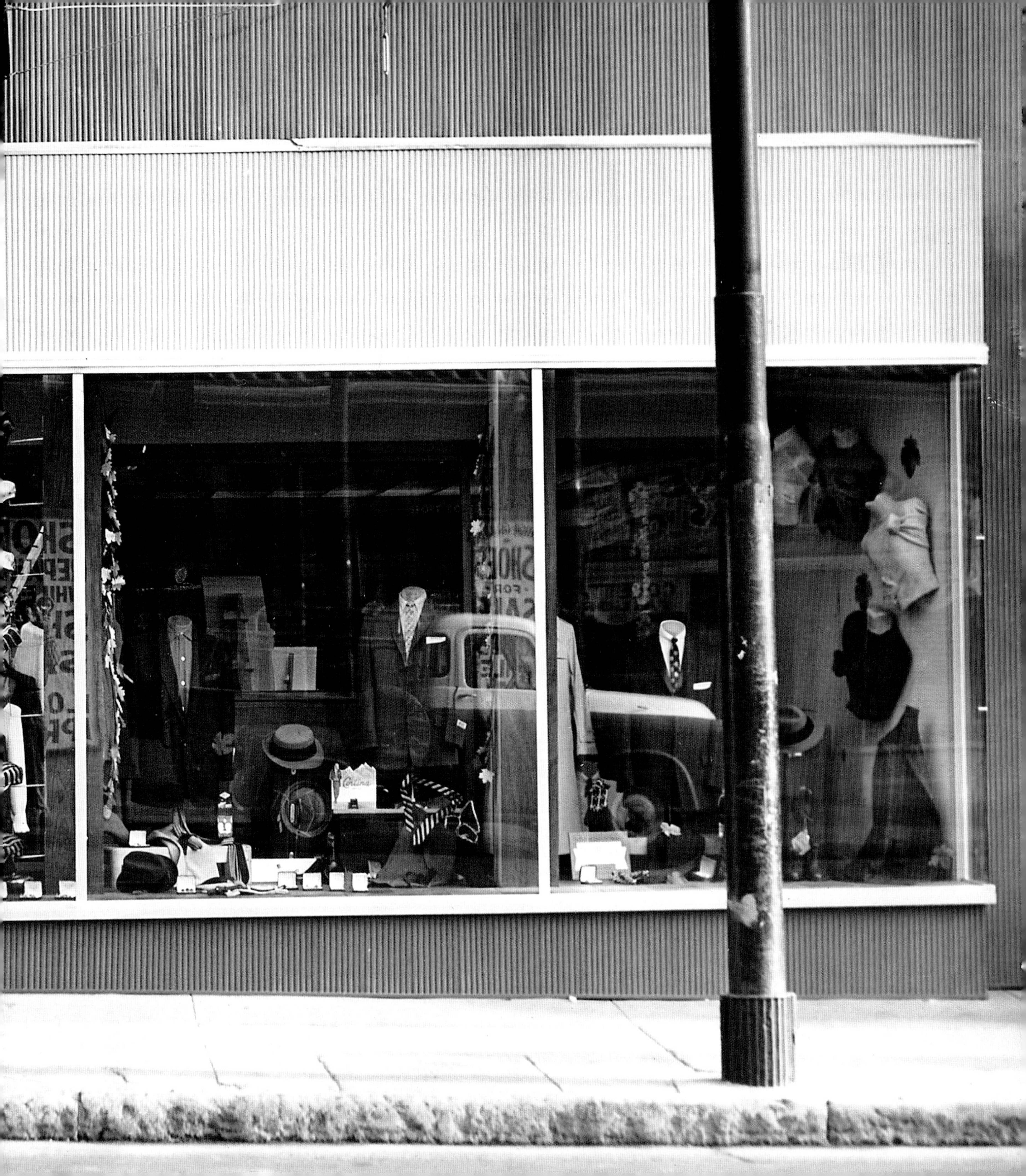

LANSKY BROTHERS: *CLOTHIER TO THE KING*

Part Two

THE KING'S NEW CLOTHES

1952–1977

IN THE SPRING OF 1952, BERNARD LANSKY noticed a gangly teenage boy hanging out in front of Lansky Brothers, gawking at the clothing in the window. The boy—on break from his job as an usher at Loews State Theater around the corner on Main Street—was sporting a greasy light-brown pompadour and wearing a movie theater uniform. He was white, an anomaly among the black entertainers that frequented Beale Street. "He was a good-looking young man," remembers Bernard. "He had that hair in ducktails, and he stood out even then."

The boy turned out to be seventeen-year-old Elvis Presley. One day, Bernard invited him in, offering to outfit Elvis in some of the store's "snazzy" clothes. The young Elvis shook his head. "No sir," he said, showing Bernard his empty pockets, "I ain't got nothing. But when I do—when I save up some money—I'm gonna come in here and buy you out."

LEFT | **Elvis's New Calling Cards**
Bernard Lansky (far left), Elvis Presley, and several members of the Memphis chapter of Lion's Club International celebrate the launch of the first Elvis Presley merchandise—including bracelets, watches, and charms—around 1956.

To that, Bernard famously replied, "Hey, do me a favor—don't buy me out. Just buy from me."

And Elvis did, eventually becoming Lansky's number one customer.

Elvis Presley wanted to stand out, both in his music and his looks, and Lansky Brothers was the only place in town where he could find clothes that would do just that. As soon as he had enough money, he purchased a shirt at Lansky's for $3.95. Later, when it came time for his junior-senior prom at L. C. Humes High School, he commissioned the store's tailors to make him a pink coat, black pants, and pink and black cummerbund. Bernard chuckles, "He always wanted to be the belle of the ball."

Elvis's style was both studied—the result of analyzing the look of the great Hollywood actors—and unique, his hair longer and blacker, his clothes louder and fancier than any of his classmates.

BELOW | For Ol' Times Sake
Elvis strikes a pose in front of the Lauderdale Courts housing in Memphis in the fall of 1954. The contrasting colors and piping on his shirt and jacket were typical Lansky styles.

A poor, quiet boy from Memphis's Lauderdale Courts apartments, he eschewed the working class styles that wealthier boys wore as a sign of rebellion. While other teenagers were wearing white T-shirts, Elvis favored vibrant silks. Instead of denim, he sported dress pants.

As his music career began to take off, so did his decades-long relationship with Lansky Brothers. Bernard outfitted Elvis for his six performances on the *Dorsey Brothers' Stage Show* and the *Louisiana Hayride*, a regional television show. Later, he put Elvis in the plaid jacket and black pants he wore for his breakthrough performance on the *Ed Sullivan Show*, as well as the black mohair suit he donned after his discharge from the army. "Anything he wanted," remembers Bernard, "We got him fitted."

And what Elvis wanted was a seemingly endless supply of clothes. He visited Lansky Brothers almost every time he was in town, always looking for something different. He liked pinks and blacks in the 1950s; suits made with silk, wool, and mohair in the 1960s; and the "superfly" look of fur and leather in the 1970s. "I never saw anyone so crazy over clothes," says Bernard.

Bernard scoured the markets and major fashion hubs to find new and interesting things for his biggest client. "I would treat him like a baby," he recalls. "Put clothes on him. Stand him in front of a mirror. And I would say, 'Elvis, this is what

BELOW | A Wild Ride
A poster promoting Elvis's April 23, 1956, appearance on the Louisiana Hayride. *The regional radio (and later, television) program broadcast local talent and had a reputation for taking chances on its performers, launching the careers of such stars as Elvis, Hank Williams, and Tex Ritter.*

ABOVE | For the Millionth and the Last Time
Elvis was a regular performer on the Louisiana Hayride *from 1954 to 1956. Lansky Brothers outfitted Elvis for all the* Hayride *shows. As Hal Lansky says, "This was when Lansky clothes began to rock 'n' roll!"*

THE KING'S NEW CLOTHES *41*

you want, right here. This is what I've got for you.' And he would start laughing and then buy it."

When Elvis's fame exploded, Bernard often opened the store at midnight so Elvis could shop in peace. And when Elvis was too busy to shop, Bernard brought truckloads of new shirts, coats, pants, hats, and shoes to his home at Graceland. His mother, Gladys Presley, would greet Bernard at the door. "They used to stay out all night on gigs," Bernard says. "They'd eat breakfast at four o'clock in the afternoon. Gladys would tell me to take the clothes up to Elvis's bedroom and come back down and eat breakfast with them." Sometimes Bernard sent his son Hal to make deliveries. The truck was usually empty when Hal returned. Elvis had purchased all the merchandise.

Yet Elvis wasn't just Lansky's best customer—he was also the store's biggest PR man. Whenever someone asked Elvis where he'd gotten an item of clothing, he made sure to give credit to Lansky Brothers. In doing so, he lured both scores of famous musicians—such as Jerry Lee Lewis, Roy Orbison, and Johnny Cash—and rabid rock 'n' roll fans to the store.

The fan frenzy didn't faze Bernard. He laughs, "They were tearing off his clothes, which was good business for us, because as soon as they tore 'em off, he had to go back and buy more." At one point, the store even became Elvis's personal post office of sorts, where adoring female fans could drop off letters to the King of Rock 'n' Roll and be assured that he would actually receive them.

Even at the height of his success, Elvis remained a true Southern gentleman, addressing Bernard as "Mr. Lansky" despite their

ABOVE | Collaring the Competition
This Lansky ad from the 1950s touted Elvis's unique style—and patronage. Bernard remembers, "To everyone who asked where he got his clothes, Elvis told them, 'At Lansky's on Beale!'"

decades-long relationship. Bernard remembers, "I told him, 'Call me Bernard.' But he always said, 'Thank you, Mr. Lansky.' He was brought up right." Elvis's manners and legendary generosity were also in full force during his shopping sprees at the store. "If you happened to be in the store while he was there, and you saw something you liked," Bernard recalls, "he'd buy it for you. It didn't matter how much it cost."

Over the years, Elvis "became a very good friend," says Bernard, "much more than a customer." Hal Lansky explains his father's friendship with Elvis: "My father will talk to anybody. It doesn't matter if they're rich or poor, black or white, famous or not. Maybe that's why he hit it off with Elvis. Elvis just knew Mr. Lansky would treat him right."

ABOVE | **Clothier to the King**
Bernard and Elvis had a familiar, easygoing relationship. Bernard recalls, "Once I said to him, 'Elvis, you can't get up there on the stage with that shaggy hair . . . Go to my barber.' Elvis wouldn't hear of it. He still had a country boy's ways."

THE KING'S NEW CLOTHES   43

Elvis on the corner of Main and Beale, a block away from Lansky Brothers. Elvis is wearing one of Lansky's most popular styles of the time: the "Mandarin," a pink collarless shirt with black piping.

Walkin' in Memphis

Early 1950s

Elvis Presley was raised on the potent, soul-moving sounds of Southern gospel. From the time he was two years old, when he scrambled from his mother's lap to sing onstage with the church choir, until his death at the age of forty-two, Elvis sang and recorded gospel music. When he moved to Memphis at age thirteen, he often visited the First Assembly of God church with his parents, where his mother's favorite group, the Blackwood Brothers, performed. He also regularly attended the all-night gospel singing sessions at Ellis Auditorium. There, he heard groups such as the Statesmen, which combined Southern gospel with traditional black gospel music.

It was this gospel influence, along with the blues that Memphis became famous for in the early-to-mid-twentieth century, which drew Elvis to the clubs and stores along Beale Street as a teenager in the 1950s. The nearly two-mile Beale Street was then a thriving hub of black culture, where blends of gospel, blues, and jazz music could be heard at every hour of the day or night. With a steady job at the Loews movie theater around the corner on Main Street, Elvis could wander Beale on his breaks, window-shopping for new and different clothes at Lansky Brothers and absorbing the styles and sounds of the black entertainers who were making music history. For Elvis Presley, a shy white boy from the poor section of town, ethnic Beale Street provided the inspiration for what would become his own unique brand of music—bluesy with a bit of black gospel, country, and, of course, rock 'n' roll.

Below: Another look at famous Beale Street in the 1950s.

Above: A 1953 Blackwood Brothers Quartet album from the Bibletone gospel label. The quartet was a favorite of Gladys Presley and a significant musical influence for Elvis.

ABOVE | Suited for Success

Bernard Lansky outfitted Elvis in the black pants, light pink coat, and pink and black cummerbund he wore to his junior-senior prom.

ABOVE | Formal Fashion

For years, a large part of the store's business came from its formal wear rentals. Many students from Elvis's alma mater, L. C. Humes High School, rented tuxedos at Lansky Brothers for their proms and other dances. Bernard often advertised in the school's yearbook, the Herald, *as seen in the image from 1957 at right.*

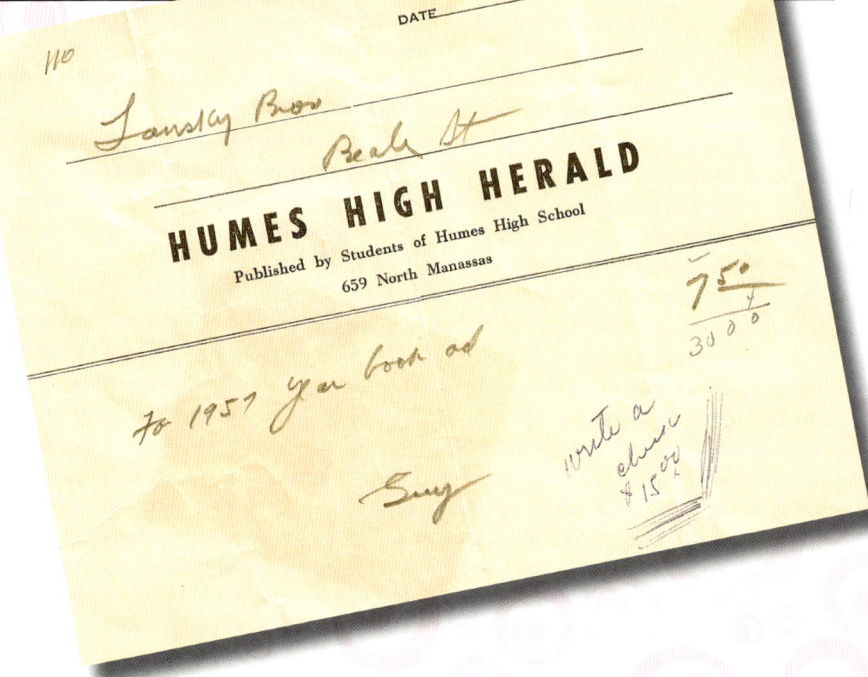

46 LANSKY BROTHERS: *CLOTHIER TO THE KING*

Elvis waits to perform at a Memphis night-club, the Eagle's Nest, in the late summer of 1954. At the time, Elvis's black and white shoes were a novelty.

Dewey Phillips and Elvis clown around inside Lansky Brothers, trying on wide-brimmed hats. Phillips was the first deejay to play Elvis's music on the radio. A spokesman for Lansky Brothers, he often exhorted his listeners to buy from the store, saying, "Come on, good people! Do like me and pay for 'em when you're wearing 'em out, or when they catch up with you, dee-gaaaawww! And be sure and tell 'em Phillips sent you!"

LEFT | Red, Hot, and Blue
A 1956 invoice from RKO records shows the amount Lansky Brothers paid to have Dewey Phillips broadcast live spots from the store during his radio show "Red, Hot, and Blue."

ABOVE | Shoppin' Around
Radio personality Dewey Phillips shops at Lansky Brothers in this previously unpublished photo.

> *"Sam Phillips recorded Elvis,*
> *Dewey Phillips played Elvis music,*
> *And Bernard Lansky clothed Elvis.*
> *Together, they changed the world."*
> —Jerry Schilling, author and member of the Memphis Mafia

THE KING'S NEW CLOTHES 49

Elvis at Lansky Brothers in the mid-1950s. Contrary to popular belief, Elvis had a narrow waistline—made seemingly smaller by his linebacker shoulders—until the last few years of his life. "I still remember his size," says Bernard. "At that time it was a 42-inch coat with a 32-inch waist, and a size 10 1/2 boot. He wore a medium shirt: 15 1/2 by 34."

GIVING CREDIT
Mid-1950s

Above: An early stage performance, circa 1955. Elvis often wore high-collared shirts such as this to show off his ducktail.

When Elvis Presley began frequenting Lansky Brothers, he didn't have the means to purchase stylish, tailored clothes. Though he worked long hours at the movie theater—and later doing gigs for Memphis radio shows, jamborees, and regional fairs—any extra money he had usually went to help feed and clothe his family. Like other poor kids from Memphis, if he wanted a snazzy shirt or a fine pair of dress pants, he had to save his money.

That all changed one day in the mid-1950s, when Elvis walked into Lansky Brothers and told Bernard Lansky that he was going to be on TV. "Mr. Lansky," he said, "design me a wardrobe that no one will forget."

Bernard, of course, was delighted to help. "I got him dressed and told him how much it was," he recalls. "But Elvis said, 'I got a problem. I don't have money yet.' I told him, 'Yes, that is a problem. But I'll tell you what, I'm going to float you the money. Just remember me when you're famous.' That was the key in the lock for him and me."

Elvis Presley always remembered Bernard Lansky's generosity, repaying Bernard with his business many times over. And Bernard would never forget Elvis's loyalty. "I was the first one to give him a charge account," he remembers proudly. "I figured he'd do something, so I took a gamble. He did all right, and so did I."

With three brands under the Lansky name and more than six decades of successful business, no one would dispute that.

Below: An invoice dated from October 30, 1956, shows twelve pieces of clothing that Lansky Brothers ordered for Elvis. The total cost: $142.80.

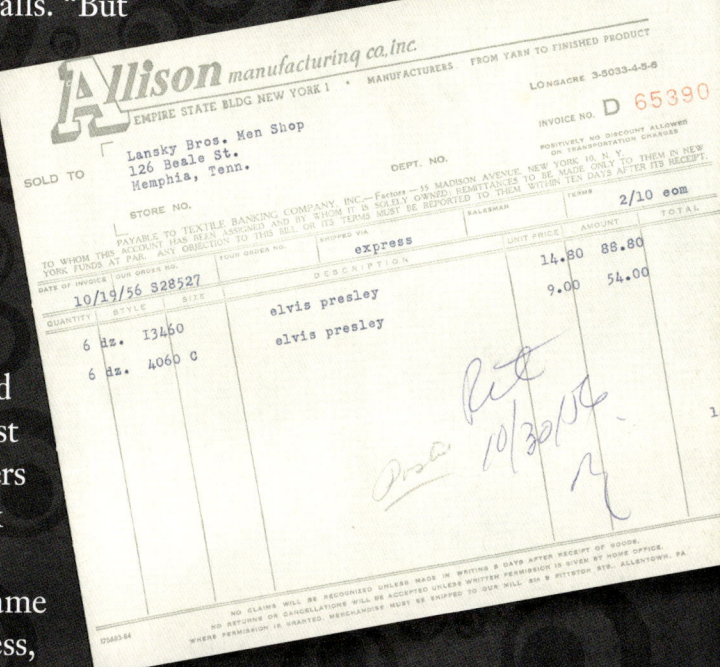

THE KING'S NEW CLOTHES   51

RIGHT AND BELOW | Record Hits

Elvis listens to albums on a phonograph. Lansky Brothers sold such phonograph machines during its early days as an army surplus store, as shown in the advertisement below.

"Elvis told me that he felt Lansky Brothers was very important early in his career in supplying him with stage wear. He wanted to look different—he did not want to look country and western. He never forgot that Bernard helped him buy clothing when he did not have a lot of money."

—George Klein, media personality and member of the Memphis Mafia

52 LANSKY BROTHERS: *CLOTHIER TO THE KING*

Elvis matches shirts to his tweed coat on a shopping spree in 1956.

THE KING'S NEW CLOTHES

the "next sharp outfit" for Elvis to wear on Ed Sullivan. "If [it's] possible to make [a] casual remark about Lansky Brothers men's shop on famous Beale Street," they wrote, "[we] would appreciate it." The receipt from their Dallas hotel is seen below.

the lone holdout. Elvis and his gyrating pelvis, Ed Sullivan maintained, were much too provocative and sensationalistic for family television. Sullivan held onto his morals . . . until Elvis sang for Sullivan's competitor, the *Steve Allen Show*, and beat him in a ratings landslide.

Sullivan put his misgivings aside and promised Elvis the then-astronomical sum of $50,000 to do three shows. The first was scheduled for September 9, 1956, and it was destined to be Elvis's biggest moment yet. *Ed Sullivan* was the top rated show in the country, one that families invariably gathered to watch together every Sunday night. With millions of viewers each week, most entertainers regarded the show as the top rung on the ladder of success. Elvis realized he needed the right clothes for such an event, so he headed straight to Lansky Brothers in Memphis. "Elvis knew that we had nothing but sharp merchandise—way out merchandise," Bernard Lansky recalls. Bernard made a special trip to New York's famed garment district, selecting

Above: Elvis in a 1956 appearance on the Ed Sullivan Show, *with drummer D. J. Fontana and bassist Bill Black in the background.*

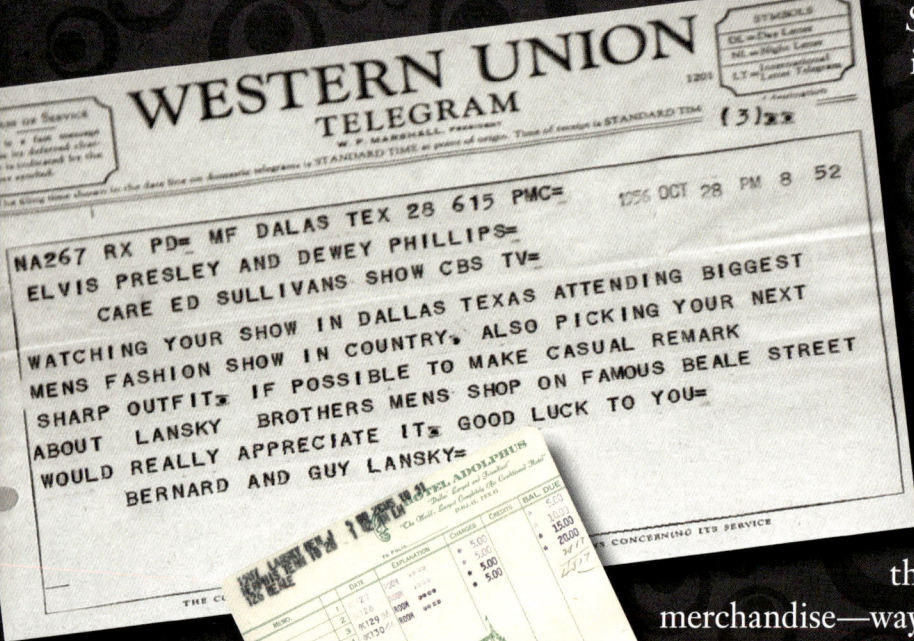

black pants, shirts in bright colors, and three sport coats for Elvis to choose from. "We knew he should be wearing something different from what other entertainers were wearing. We tried everything on him and made doggone sure he looked right, 'cause on stage you've got to make a presentation."

In the end, Elvis donned black trousers with a plaid jacket—an outfit that stood out even on the black-and-white TVs of the time. Despite mostly being filmed from the waist up to censor his "provocative" hip-swiveling, Elvis captured the attention of a record sixty million people, more than 80 percent of the viewing audience, as he sang "Don't Be Cruel," "Love Me Tender," "Ready Teddy," and "Hound Dog."

That Sunday evening at eight o'clock, Bernard was working—as usual. "We had the TV set on in the store," he recalls, "and it shocked me when I saw him. I thought, 'Man, this boy is dynamite.' As soon as he was finished, I knew he was on his way."

Above: Elvis ignited a fan frenzy after his first appearance on the Ed Sullivan Show *wearing a fashionable plaid Lansky sports jacket that Bernard had selected for him.*

As Elvis's fame soared, so did the numbers of people who came to Lansky Brothers. This enormous postcard was set up inside the store for fans to send messages to Elvis for Christmas in 1961.

ABOVE AND ABOVE RIGHT | Memorable Merchandise

Whatever Elvis touched became as golden as his famous lamé suit. Some of the more obscure merchandise he licensed included a pink head scarf with his likeness and autograph, and hats that featured comic-book-style illustrations and lyrics from his songs. Bernard is pictured wearing one of the hats above.

LEFT | Going Postal

During the 1950s and 1960s, Lansky Brothers acted as a post office of sorts for Elvis's fans, who sent letters to the store that were addressed both to "Elvis's clothiers" and to Elvis himself.

THE KING'S NEW CLOTHES   57

Elvis shopping with Bernard in the early 1960s. To accommodate Elvis's schedule—and rising star—Bernard began opening Lansky Brothers at odd hours. At other times, he or his son Hal brought clothing to Elvis at Graceland.

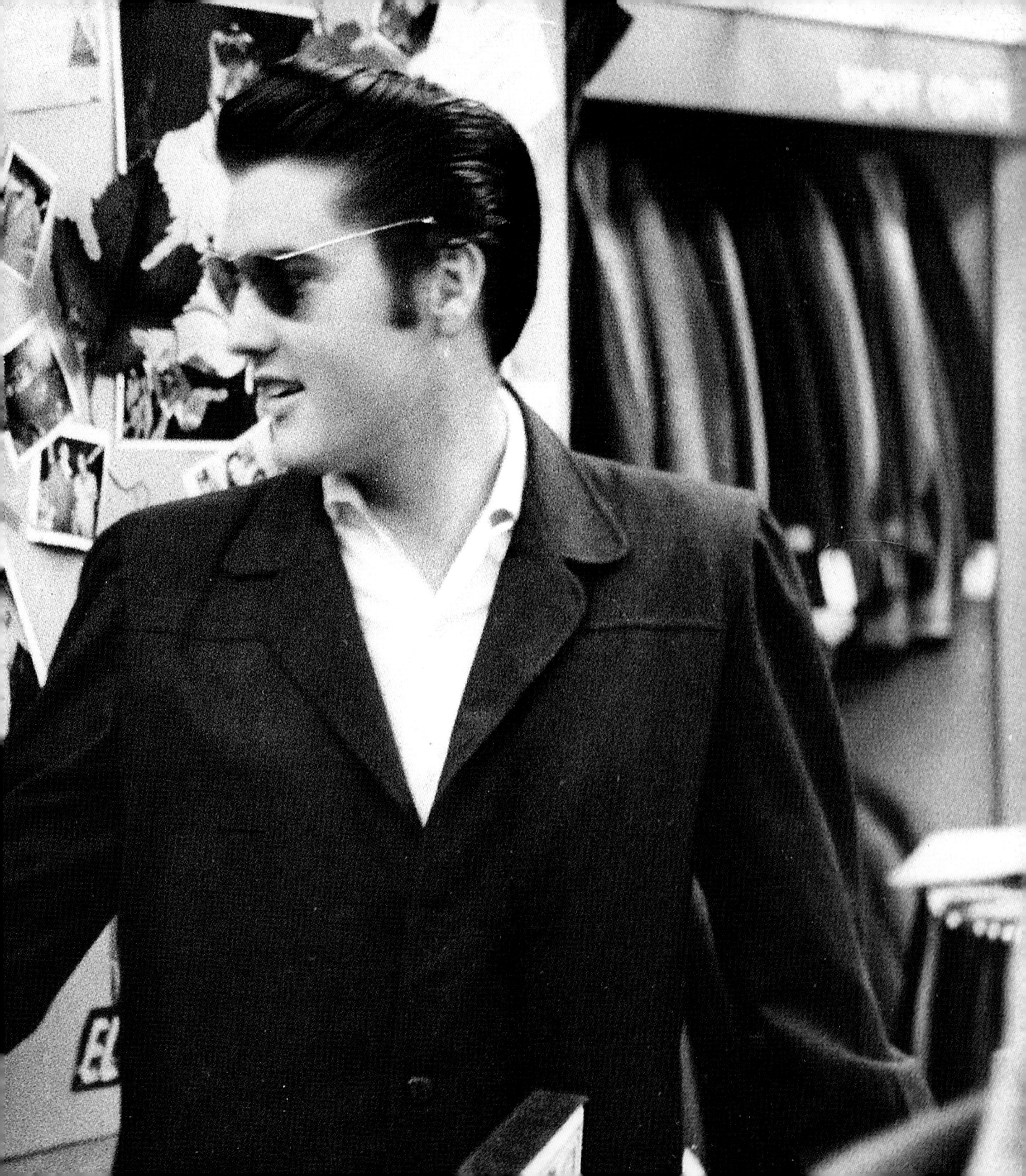

The Sloppiest Dresser in America?

1956

While Elvis—and Bernard Lansky—thought he looked sharp, not everyone agreed. In 1956, the same year Elvis exploded onto the scene with performances on the *Steve Allen Show* and the *Ed Sullivan Show*, the Custom Tailors Guild of America published its list of the country's "Ten Best-Dressed Men." Not only was Elvis conspicuously left off the list, he was also blasted by the guild's chairman.

The *Memphis Press-Scimitar* quoted the chairman as saying, "I think there ought to be a law—or public pressure at least—requiring Elvis Presley, Marlon Brando, and Ted Williams—to name just a few of our sloppier celebrities—to dress properly."

Bernard Lansky and his brother Guy promptly fired back. They reminded the paper that they not only dressed Elvis Presley, but they also outfitted Little Richard, Warren Smith, "Fats" Domino, and other big name "rock 'n' rollers." They knew what entertainers needed to wear to get noticed.

"We're really going to let that Custom Tailors Guild have it . . ." said Guy Lansky. "Via telegram." The telegram said:

"Please be advised in regard to a wire service release to the daily newspapers throughout the country that ELVIS PRESLEY is NOT—in your term—'one of the worst-dressed men in the country.' We, Lansky Bros., are the sole suppliers of Elvis Presley's clothes. We feel that we

Above: Elvis rides one of his Harley-Davidson motorcycles in white pants with a white high-collared shirt.

Below: A pair of Elvis's white ankle boots with side zippers, stuffed with a scarf. Both the shoes and the scarf are from Lansky Brothers.

Above: Elvis looks over the merchandise in Lansky Brothers, while Bernard (far left), Guy (closest to Elvis), and other staff members bring him clothing. Bernard and Guy not only took the Custom Tailors Guild to task for calling Elvis "sloppy," they also drafted a letter to Bing Crosby, who publicly criticized the King's wardrobe.

have made Elvis Presley on the merit of his clothes. Our clothes are all fair trade items by all famous national brand shops.

"Although Elvis may not be the most conservative dresser, he is definitely not sloppy. Ted Williams and Marlon Brando just don't give a dern, but EP has to have everything just so. Every stitch down the sides of the 40 pairs of pegged slacks has to be a contrasting color.

"He's changed—blue suede shoes are out, now he likes white shoes, continental style with double stitching and thick soles. His favorite colors were pink and black, now they're black and white."

They concluded, "Don't let anybody fool you, that kid's a sharp dresser. Some of his outfits are out of this world."

Left: A pair of Elvis's royal blue A-1 pegger pants, hanging on a vintage Lansky hanger. Elvis loved to modify his clothes, as seen in the V on the pant bottoms here.

THE KING'S NEW CLOTHES 61

ABOVE | Jailbird Stripes
A 1957 publicity shot for Jailhouse Rock *shows Elvis wearing a Lansky jacket.*

ABOVE | The Stars Align
Elvis dated a string of Hollywood starlets, including Natalie Wood of Rebel Without a Cause. *They were spotted all over Memphis when Wood came for a visit, even dropping into Lansky Brothers to shop.*

"My favorite hobby is *collecting these real cool outfits*. I'd almost rather wear them than eat."
—*Elvis Presley*

62   LANSKY BROTHERS: *CLOTHIER TO THE KING*

Elvis records the title song to the movie Jailhouse Rock *at Radio Recorders in Hollywood, May 1957.*

THE KING'S NEW CLOTHES

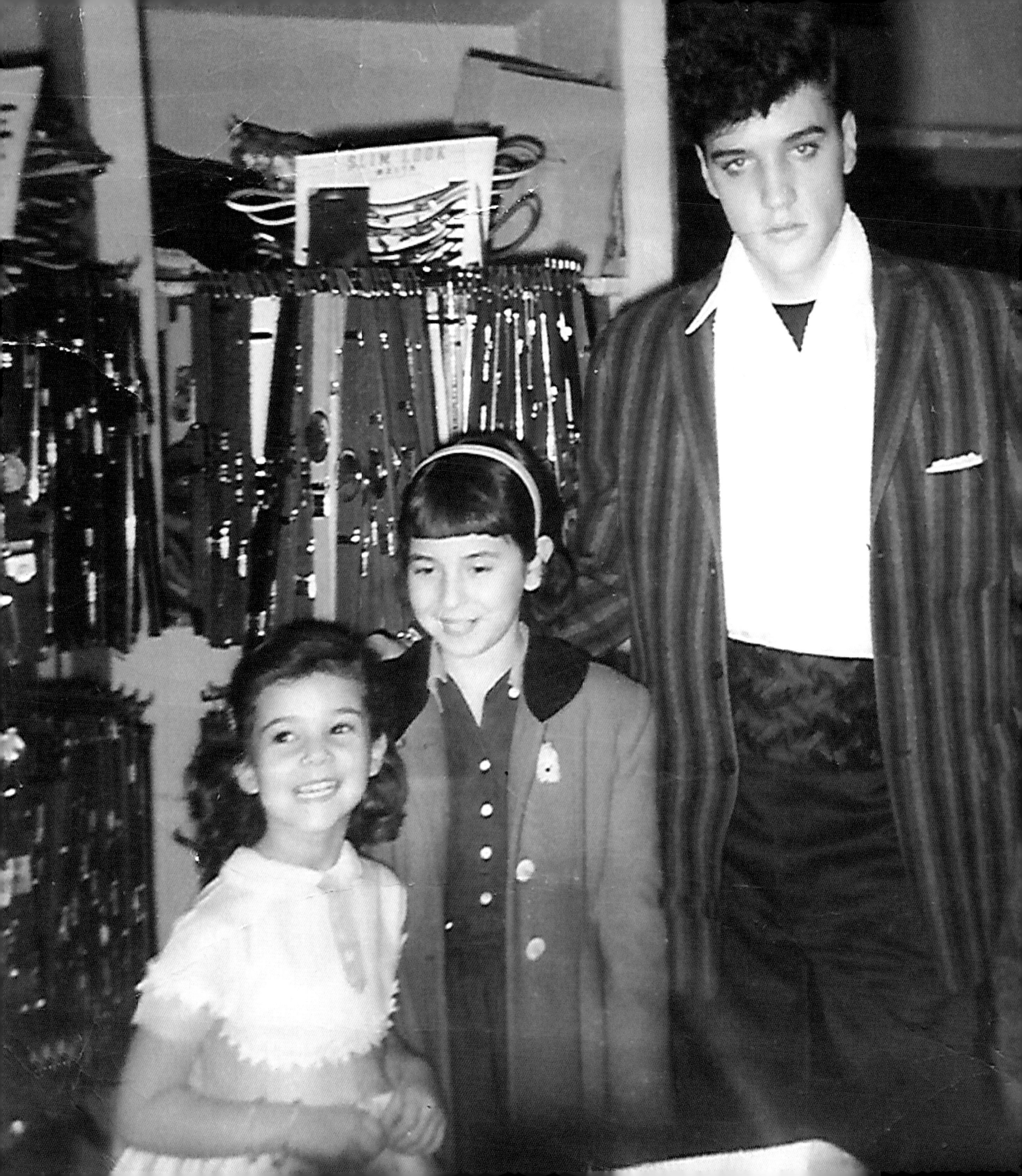
SLIM LOOK

LEFT | Soulful Style
Elvis always preferred clothing that was a little bit different, as evidenced by the stripes on this Lansky jacket. Few of Elvis's clothes from this period can be found in the archives of his estate. Some people believe that his clothing was given away, possibly when he moved to Graceland. Others speculate that Elvis's manager Colonel Parker had the King's old clothes cut into squares and put in the sleeves of his albums for a promotion with RCA.

BELOW | Getting Tagged
Lansky Brothers had these labels sewn into clothes that were specifically made for Elvis.

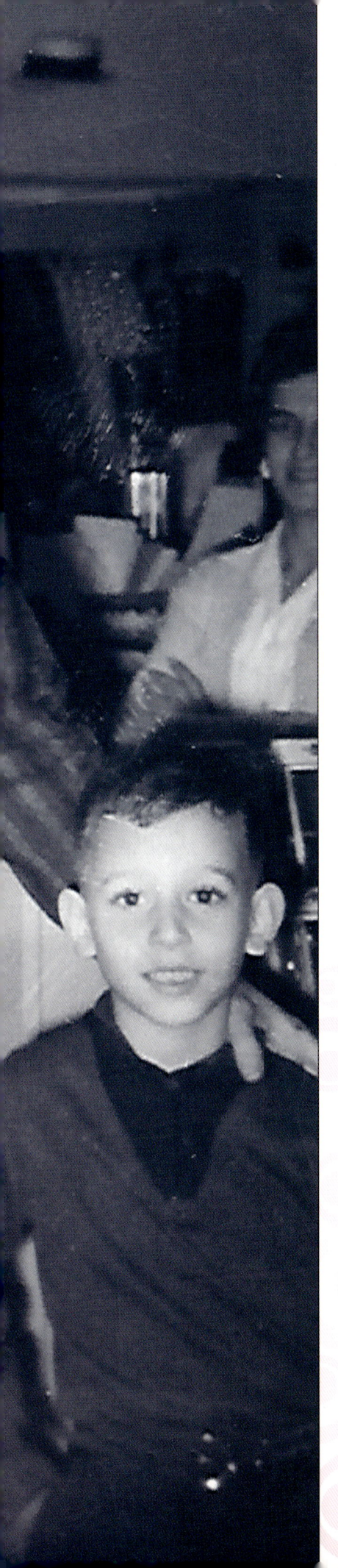

LEFT | Rock 'n' Roll Heritage
Several members of the Lansky family with Elvis in 1956 (left to right): Anise Lansky, Hal's sister; family friend Cathy Malkin; and Hal Lansky. Bernard's sister Mildred is in the background. The cummerbund, pocket square, and black T-shirt under the white dress shirt are classic Lansky style.

THE KING'S NEW CLOTHES 65

Elvis tends to his Messerschmitt in June 1956. Elvis had a lifelong love of fancy cars and motorcycles, collecting dozens of vehicles—including a pink Cadillac, red MG, 1975 Dino Ferrari, and several Harley-Davidson motorcycles.

Mr. Lansky's New Car
1957

Elvis Presley's gift giving was as extravagant as his taste in clothing. Whether buying clothes for total strangers, contributing to local causes, or bankrolling his large entourage—which included many of his childhood friends—his generosity was legendary.

Bernard Lansky witnessed Elvis's thoughtfulness on countless occasions in the store, but he never imagined he would be on the receiving end of it. "Then he walked into the store one day," Bernard remembers, "and said, 'Come look what I've got.'"

A rare German Messerschmitt car was parked on the street, a gift from Elvis's record label at the time, RCA. The automaker, which had built aircraft for Germany during World War II, had been forbidden from manufacturing airplanes after the war. So as an alternative, it produced the Messerschmitt, a three-wheeled bubble/motorcycle car that opened on top.

"It was burgundy outside, black inside—like an airplane without the wings," Bernard recalls. "I said, 'Elvis that's a nice one. When you get tired of it, I want it. That's mine.'"

Not long after, Elvis approached Bernard. "I'll make you a deal," he said. "You let me pick out all the clothes I want in here and you can have the car."

Bernard readily agreed, giving Elvis free run of the store. Later, Elvis recalled of the incident, "I was in there about two hours, and the store was a wreck when I left."

For Bernard, however, it was worth it. "That car was something," he says. "I still have it."

Above: Bernard in the car gifted to him by Elvis, with his son Hal in the backseat. Elvis traded the car in exchange for a two-and-a-half hour shopping spree at Lansky Brothers.

Below: The title of Elvis's Messerschmitt shows the King's receipt of the car in March 1956 and the transfer into Bernard's name in August 1957.

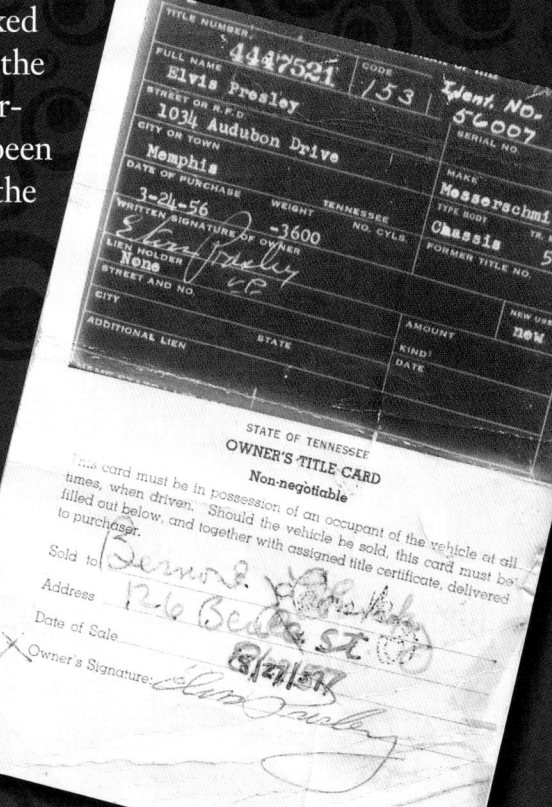

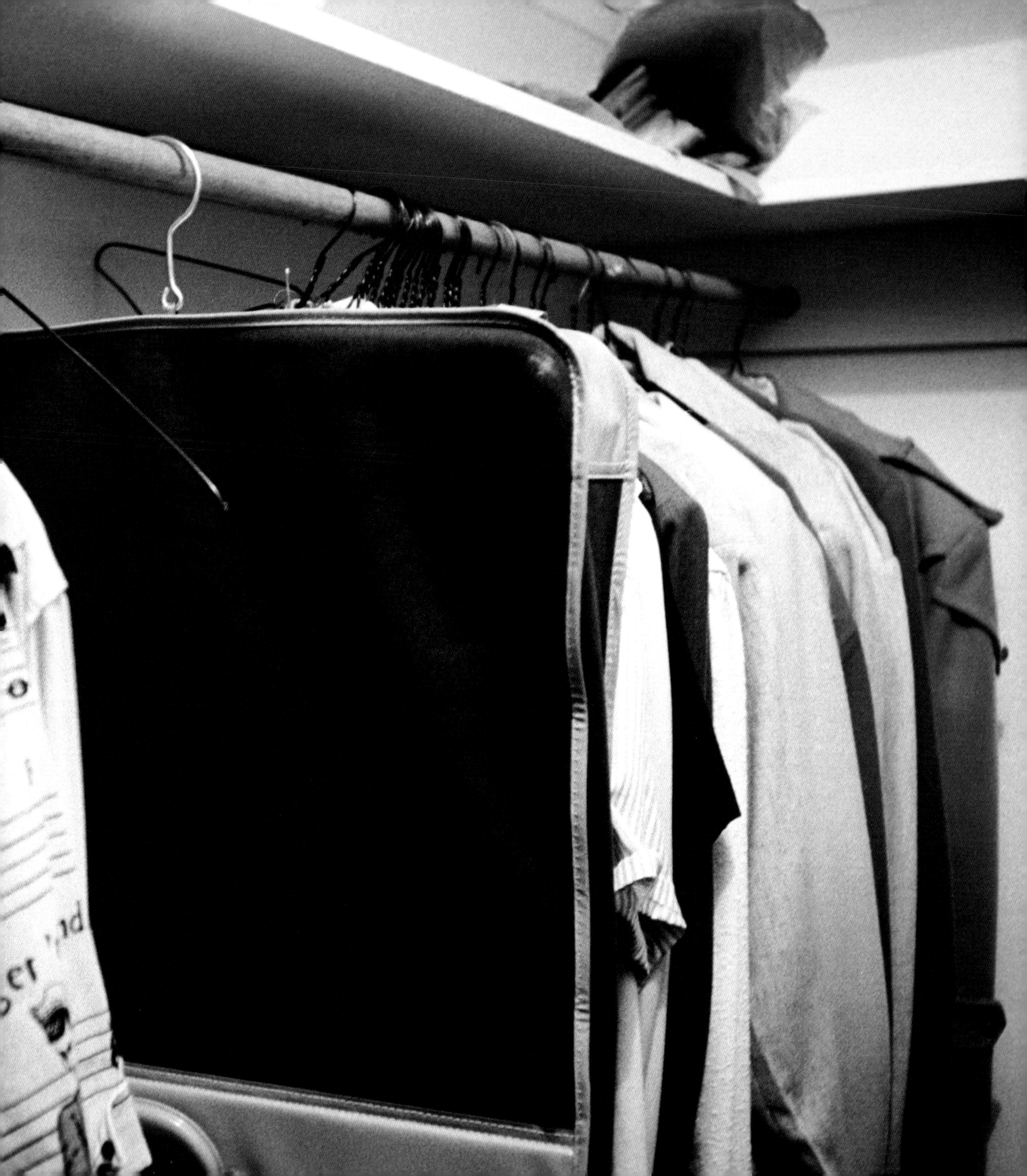

An inside look at Elvis's closet in the 1950s. Several Lansky jackets are hanging on the right.

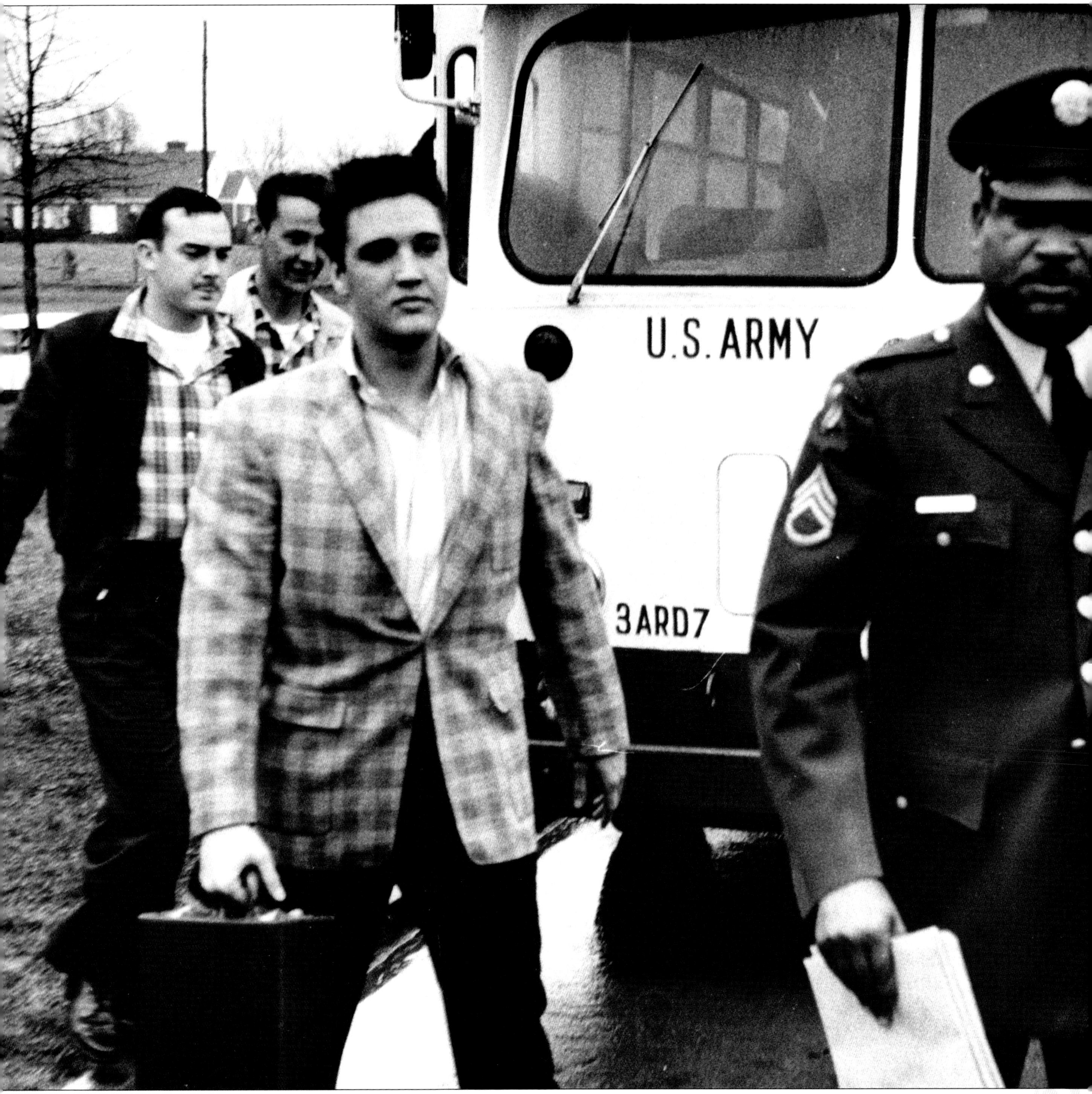
U.S. ARMY
3ARD7

LEFT | Jacket Required
Bernard received this letter from one of Elvis's friends just a few days after attending the draft board signing. Like his millions of fans, even the King's friends wanted to dress like him.

Judith Spreckels
5126 Ledge Avenue, Burbank, California

March 28, 1958

Lansky Bros.
126 Beale St.
Memphis, Tenn.

Dear Mr. Lansky,

I met you Monday morning at the draft board when Elvis Presley was signing in, and you gave me your card.

I was presented with a jacket from your store by a mutual friend of Elvis' and mine. I had been wanting a jacket like that since I had worn Elvis' all the time when he was in Calif. My gift jacket was beige with brown knit collar and sleeves. Elvis' jacket is powder blue with white sleeves and collar. Apparently you did not have a powder blue with white, so my friend bought the beige. It is very nice and I like it extremely well, so well, in fact, that I would still like the jacket in blue with the white sleeves and collar.

The jacket is manufactured by "HOLMAN" of Calif. I wear a 36 in this jacket. Please inform me of the other color combinations this jacket comes in, also the price, and how long it will take to get me the blue and white one. Please send me that information as soon as possible, and order the jacket immediately regardless of price. I hope I have described the jacket sufficiently. The solid portion of the jacket feels like felt-velvet combination. It has a zipper front and is lined throughout. Thank you for your prompt attention to this matter.

Sincerely
Judy Spreckels

LEFT | Soldier Boy
Elvis was inducted into the U.S. Army on March 24, 1958, accompanied by a small group of family and friends, wearing the plaid Lansky jacket he'd donned for his breakout performance on the Ed Sullivan Show. *The air force and navy had also offered unique bids for his services, but Elvis turned them down, wanting to be a regular G.I.*

> "I never saw anyone *so crazy over clothes.*
> Elvis was a real sharp dresser. Real neat.
> His clothes looked great on him. *He was clean as Ajax.*"
> —Bernard Lansky

THE KING'S NEW CLOTHES 71

RIGHT | Hometown Hero
Elvis stops into Lansky Brothers to select an outfit for his July 4, 1956, benefit concert at Russwood Park stadium in Memphis. The concert played to fourteen thousand screaming fans.

BELOW | Custom Clothier
A label from Lansky Brothers's new line, Clothier to the King, recreates the look of Elvis and makes it available to modern-day shoppers.

RIGHT | Cool Cats—and Caps
This ad from the 1950s, geared toward Beale Street musicians, trumpeted various popular styles, including "the DJ's all-time favorite" Dial-Twister cap and the Bo-Jazz shirt shown in "black for impact!"

72   LANSKY BROTHERS: *CLOTHIER TO THE KING*

Elvis's performance at Russwood Park in 1956 was one of the venue's most famous non-baseball events. A few years later, the stadium was destroyed by a fire.

RIGHT | Flipping for Fashion

Bernard Lansky first flipped Elvis's collar to show off his ducktail. Now, says Bernard, "There isn't a day that goes by that someone doesn't ask me to flip his collar like I did for Elvis!"

BELOW | Mod Menswear

This Lansky ad reflected the swinging styles that were popular in the mid to late 1960s. The modern "mod" look came from Carnaby Street and King's Road in London, and included bell-bottom pants, loud, geometric patterns, and bright colors.

"I would treat him like a baby. Put clothes on him. Stand him in front of a mirror. And I would say, 'Elvis, this is what you want, right here. This is what I've got for you.' And he would start laughing, then buy it."

—Bernard Lansky

74   LANSKY BROTHERS: *CLOTHIER TO THE KING*

Bernard fits Elvis in a topcoat in this photo from the early 1960s. Elvis was fond of captain's hats, famously wearing one in his 1962 movie Girls! Girls! Girls!

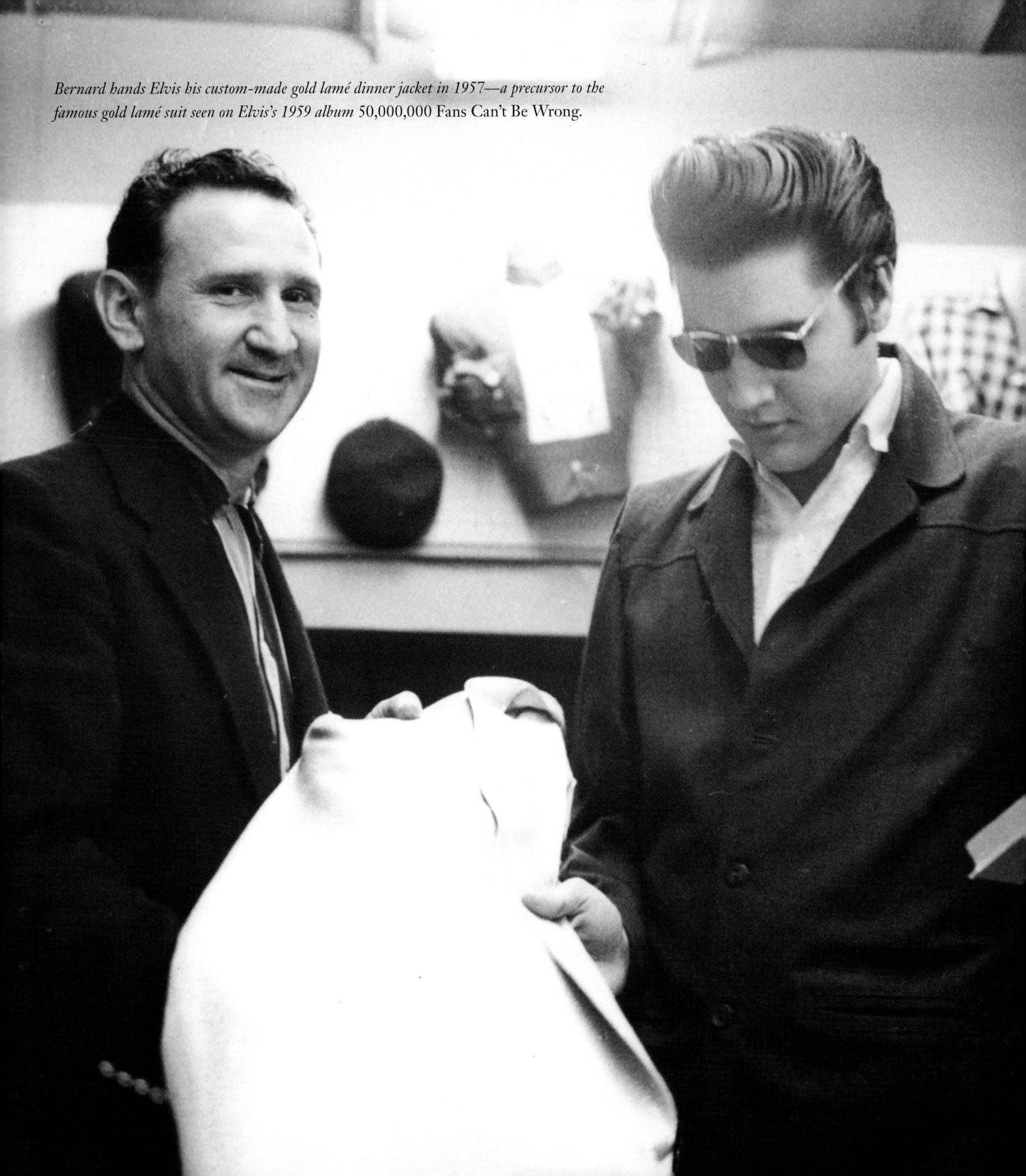

Bernard hands Elvis his custom-made gold lamé dinner jacket in 1957—a precursor to the famous gold lamé suit seen on Elvis's 1959 album 50,000,000 Fans Can't Be Wrong.

```
                                              SHOWROOMS
                                              NEW YORK: 200 FIFTH AVE.
                                              LOS ANGELES: 860 S. LOS ANGELES ST.
                                              CHICAGO: LYTTON BUILDING

                     After Six
                      BY RUDOFKER

S. RUDOFKER'S SONS INC., 22ND & MARKET STS., PHILADELPHIA 3, PA. • LOcust 4-2471


          January 2, 1957


          Lansky Bros. Mens Shop
          126 Beale Avenue
          Memphis, Tennessee

                        Attn:  Guy & Bernard Lansky

          Dear Boys:

          Thanks very much for sending along that photo of
          Elvis Presley receiving his gold Lame dinner
          jacket.

          I'm turning this over to our Publicity Department
          in New York and hope something will come through
          on it.

          Best wishes for a very Happy Holiday.


          Cordially,
          S. RUDOFKER'S SONS INC.


          SAM RUDOFKER

          SR:ALG
```

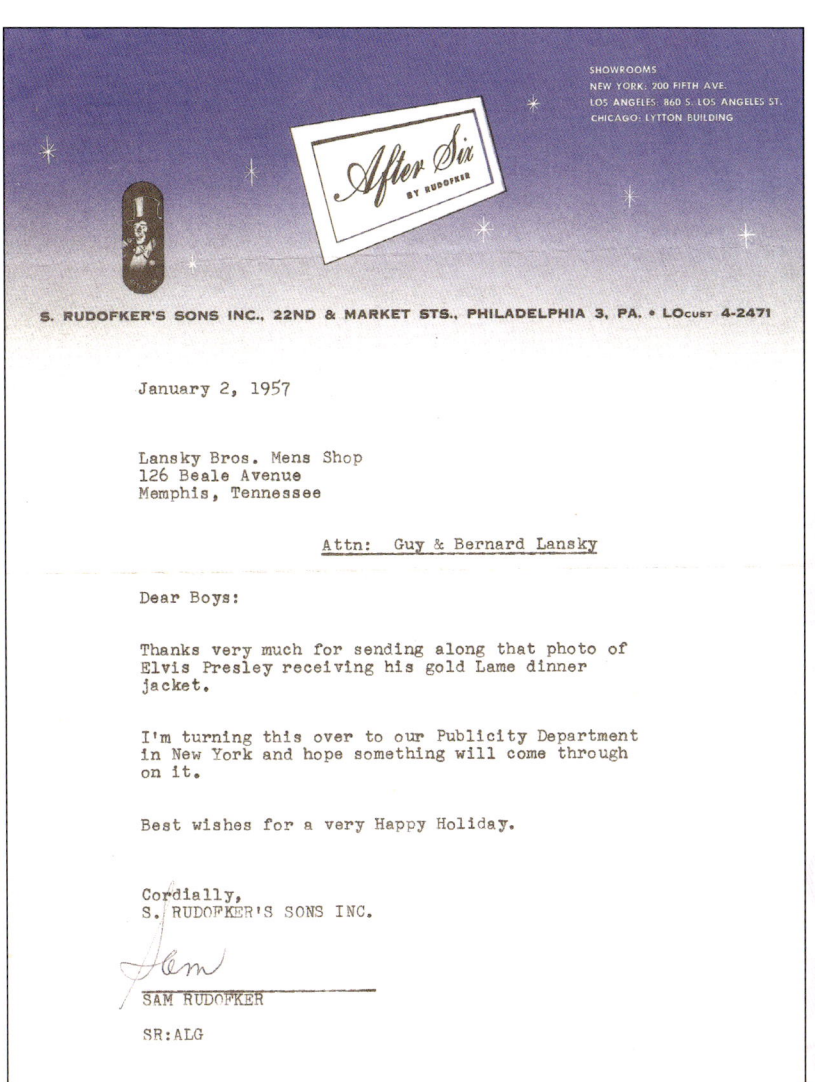

ABOVE | All That Glitters

The maker "After Six by Rudofker" created Elvis's gold lamé jacket, sold to him by Lansky Brothers. This letter from Sam Rudofker, dated January 2, 1957, thanks Bernard and Guy for sending a photo of Elvis receiving the jacket.

THE KING'S NEW CLOTHES

RIGHT | Unforgettable Elvis
A reproduction of an advertisement done by Elvis Presley Enterprises in 2002 to promote Lansky's Elvis-inspired clothing line, Clothier to the King. It featured Elvis's famous words to Bernard Lansky.

BELOW | A Mod World
This Lansky ad from the 1960s showcases a British suit "with the Bolero look" from the store's mod line, available in black . . . and iridescent gold, blue-gold, and olive-gold.

"Mr. Lansky, design me a wardrobe no one will forget."

"I remember one year Priscilla Presley came into the store before Christmas. It was right after she and Elvis got married. She wanted to purchase a leather coat for Elvis but didn't have enough money with her, so she put two dollars down to hold it on layaway!"

—Bernard Lansky

78 LANSKY BROTHERS: *CLOTHIER TO THE KING*

TELEGRAM RECEIVED BY TELEPHONE	
Recopy	DATE LL MAY 4 1214P
MR AND MRS ELVIS PRESLEY	CHECK CGN 12PD
GRACELAND HIGHWAY 51 S	TEL. NO. 525 5401
148	DEST'N MFS
HEARTIEST CONGRATUOATIONS AND BEST WISHES FOR A LONG AND HAPPY LIFE TOGETHER	SIGNATURE GUY AND BERNARD LANSKY
	SUB. LANSKY BROS MENS SHOP

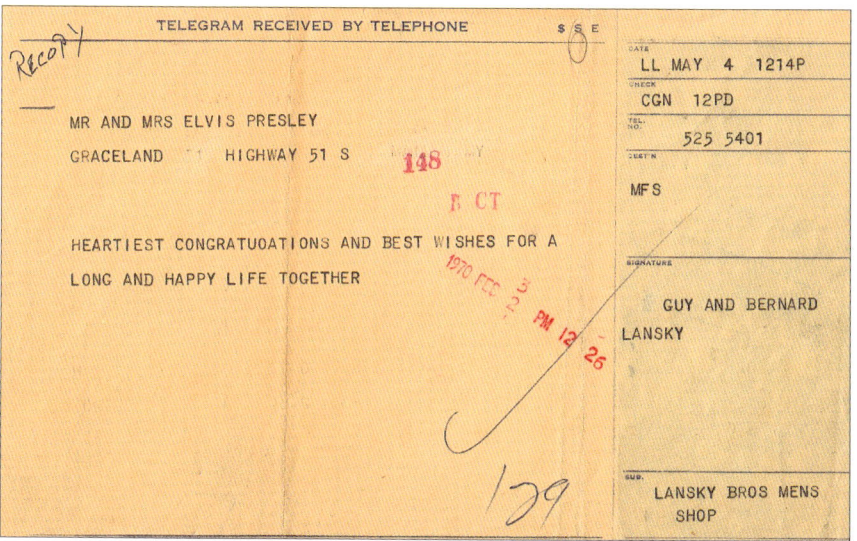

ABOVE AND LEFT | A Thing Called Love

Elvis and Priscilla Beaulieu Presley on their wedding day, May 1, 1967. Bernard and Guy Lansky sent the newlyweds this congratulatory telegram, left, a few days later.

THE KING'S NEW CLOTHES

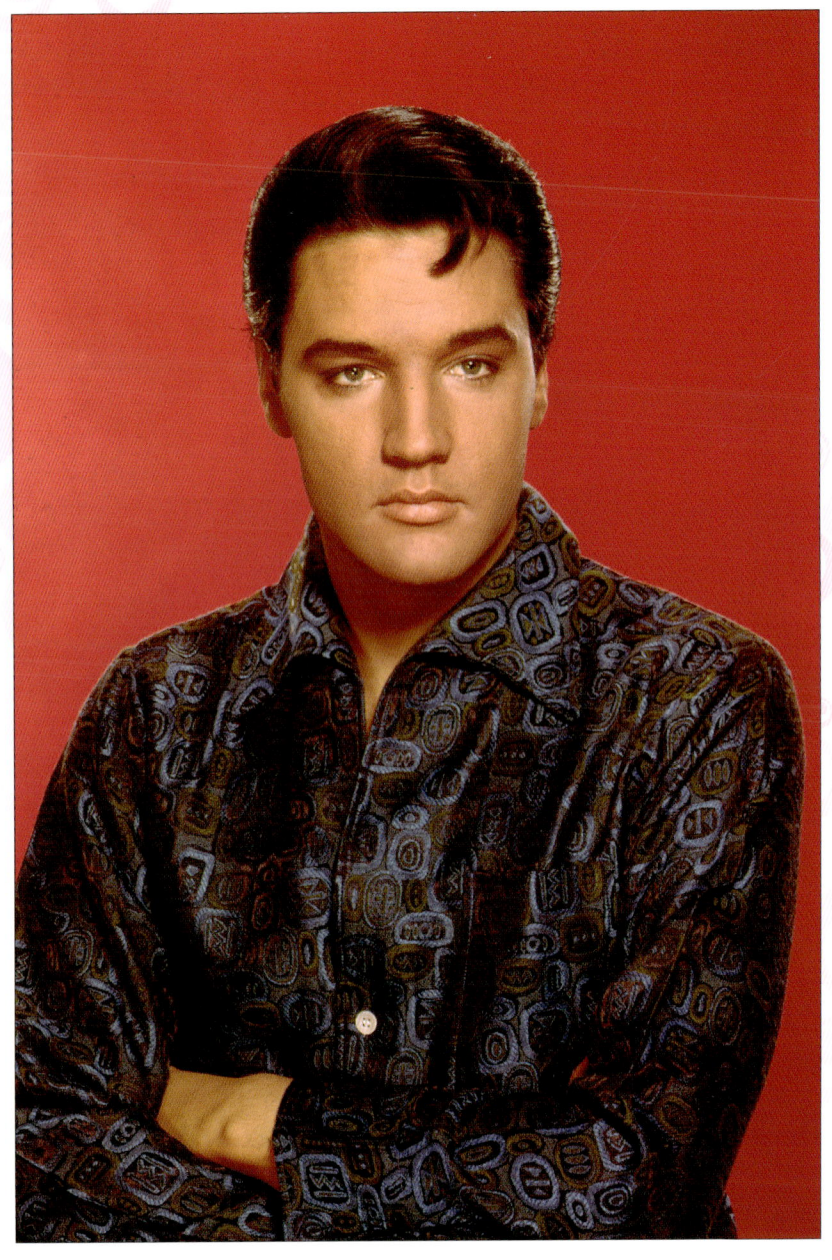

ABOVE | Bright Future

Elvis loved wearing color, and the brighter the better. He purchased many of his patterned silk shirts, like the ones in the publicity shot above left and in the casual photo above right, at Lansky Brothers.

RIGHT | Fit for a King

These wide-banded, fur velour hats from Elvis's wardrobe were designed by Oleg Cassini for Lansky Brothers. Elvis wore size 7 3/8. The pinstriped suit at far right features a silk paisley ascot and matching pants (not shown).

Elvis was fond of collarless jackets in the 1950s and 1960s. This mandarin-style red jacket is from Lansky Brothers.

THE KING'S NEW CLOTHES

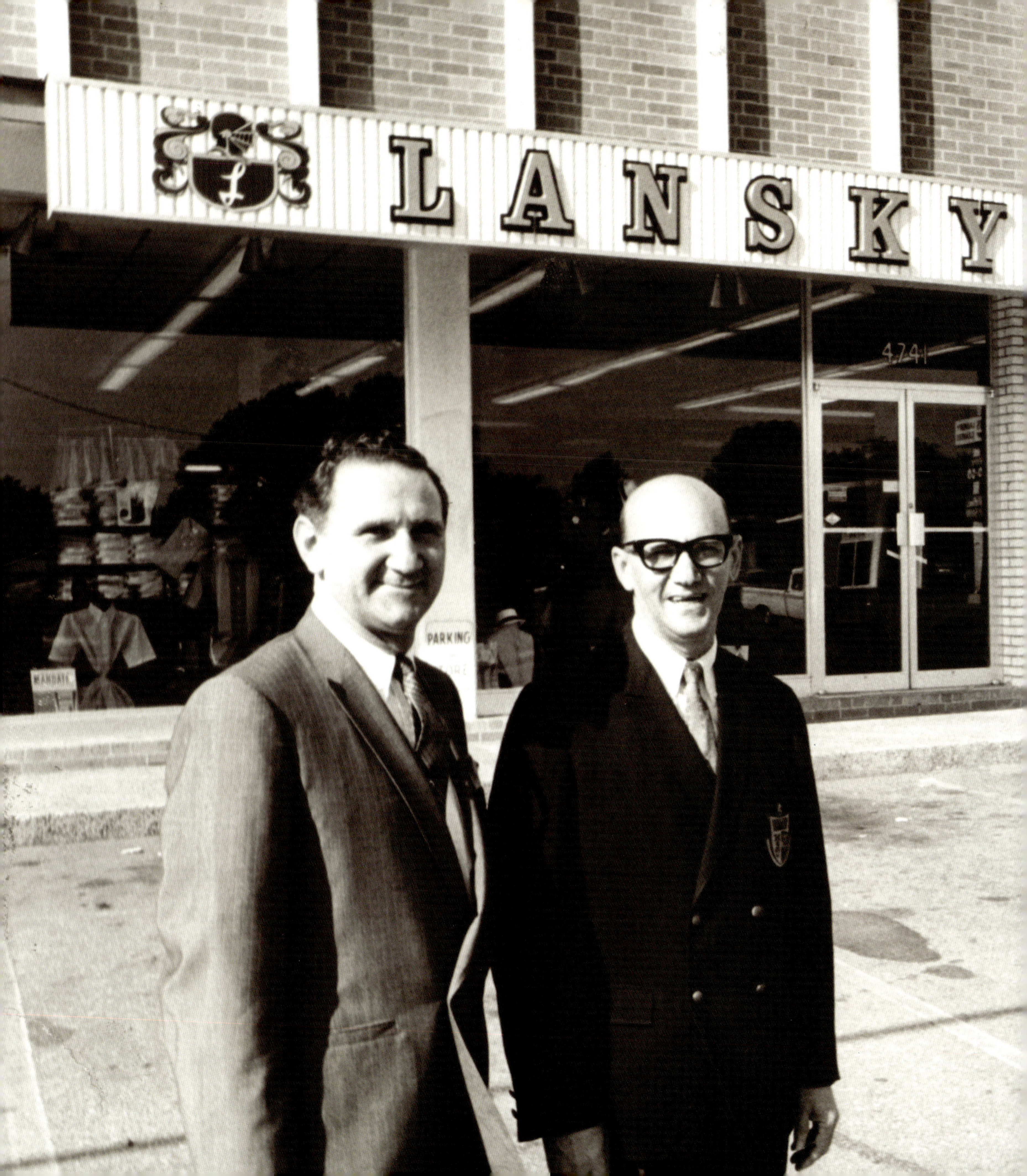
LANSKY
4741
PARKING

Bernard (left) and Guy Lansky in front of their newest shop in 1967: 4741 Poplar Avenue. In 1976, they opened a 14,500-square-foot store nearby and closed this store on Poplar shortly thereafter.

FUR TRIMMED COATS AND BLUE SUEDE SHOES
Decades of Style

Elvis Presley's lyrics and stage moves weren't the only things that shook up 1950s popular culture. His carefully crafted image—including his shoe-blackened hair and wild clothing—raised more than a few eyebrows as well.

Just as Elvis had integrated black gospel and blues into his own musical style, he also adapted the more extravagant fashions that were favored by the black entertainers on Beale Street. Unlike the Levi's and T-shirts that were popular around the mid-twentieth century, Elvis favored shiny silks, voluminous trousers, big sleeve cuffs, pegged pants, patent leather half boots, and high-collared shirts that would show off his ducktail. These types of cat clothes were all in the window at Lansky Brothers on Beale Street, which was known around Memphis as an ethnic clothing store.

It wasn't just Elvis's clothing styles that riled conservative America, though. Even his color choices stood out. Prior to Elvis, men simply didn't wear pink or black, a color combination that was considered effeminate. But once Elvis donned such clothing, such style rules went out the window. Bernard Lansky remembers, "After his early records on the Sun label began making him a local hero, all the kids swarmed us because they wanted pink and black, just like Elvis wore."

The local paper concurred, asserting that seven out of every ten young men on the street in 1950s Memphis were rolling up their sleeves, turning up their collars, and sporting both "peggers" and a ducktail. "They were looking for something different," Bernard chuckles, "and we gave it to them."

Above: A belt and two styles of blue suede shoes sold at Lansky's today. The hit song "Blue Suede Shoes," written by Carl Perkins, was the first on Elvis's groundbreaking 1956 album Elvis Presley.

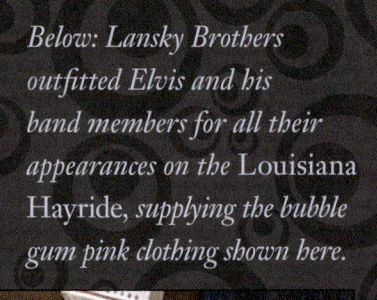

Below: Lansky Brothers outfitted Elvis and his band members for all their appearances on the Louisiana Hayride, *supplying the bubble gum pink clothing shown here.*

Right: Elvis at a 1960s-era performance. Elvis's clothing during this decade was relatively subdued, with cleaner lines, fewer patterns, and simpler styles.

Below: Lansky Brothers was responsible for introducing the colors of the 1950s—pink and black—to the world. Bernard remembers, "Elvis would drop into the store, and I'd dress him in wild combinations of his favorite colors, pink and black." It was a revolutionary look; at the time, men didn't wear pink and black. After Elvis was seen in his Lansky outfits, though, his millions of fans followed suit.

Below: Pieces of several Lansky denim patchwork suits from the 1970s—complete with fly collars, covered buttons, bell bottoms, and Swarovski crystals.

Some of Elvis's style ideas came from his own notion of what a successful performing artist should wear: attention-getting and well-groomed threads that were in no way practical. He was also inspired by Hollywood. Bernard remembers, "He would watch TV and see those gangsters wearing those big hats. We called them Dobbs hats. I think I sold them for twenty-five or thirty dollars. Elvis would call and say, 'Mr. Lansky, send me over a half-dozen of them hats. And send some over for the other guys, too.' So everybody in his entourage, which became known as the Memphis Mafia, would get a hat."

Bernard Lansky dressed Elvis through every phase of his life, from the outlandish outfits of the 1950s and the more tailored suits of the 1960s to the extravagant clothing of the 1970s. One such piece—a pink leather fur-trimmed coat that Elvis sent to Lansky Brothers for repair in 1977—still hangs in the store. Elvis had ripped the coat's back vent while getting out of his car and never returned to pick it up.

"Elvis was a real sharp dresser," Bernard says fondly. "He was clean as Ajax. I never saw anyone so crazy over clothes."

THE KING'S NEW CLOTHES 85

Elvis was as particular about his interior decor as his clothing. The Jungle Room at Graceland reflects his love of fur and the exotic.

LEFT | Guitar Man

Elvis at a recording session in the 1970s, wearing a colorful patterned shirt and black-and-white pinstriped pants. Elvis did not worry about mixing patterns and stripes as long as the colors matched.

> "He liked anything we put on him because *it was different* and it was sharp. He gave the artists the notion that they can *do what they want to do,* to not worry about what people think."
> —Bernard Lansky

RIGHT | Animal Instinct

Lansky Brothers was probably the only store of its kind to have a full-time furrier on staff who added fur collars to jackets and created custom-made mink hats. Elvis was fond of fur coats, including this full-length caramel colored leather coat with fur collar, and this black velveteen short jacket with Edwardian collar and pink lining.

THE KING'S NEW CLOTHES

RIGHT | Heavyweight Icons

Elvis with Muhammad Ali in a 1973 photo. Here, Elvis is wearing a long navy coat from Lansky Brothers with an Edwardian collar and crinkled velvet cape (also shown below).

"Elvis was like a walking PR man for us. Whenever someone asked him where he got his clothes, he'd say, At Lansky's on Beale!'"
—Bernard Lansky

RIGHT | Far-Out Fashion

An ad from the late 1960s showcases one of the more daring styles of the time: the "Bat Man Shirt-Jacket," which featured a small, detachable cape. As usual, Elvis put his own spin on the style years later, as seen in the image above.

"HOLY RAVIOULI"

Lansky BROTHERS

Is where you'll find the...

BAT MAN SHIRT-JACKET

Pick up several in blue, purple, olive or black. The bat-cape is detachable and fully lined in a darker tone. Without the cape your shirt-jacket is a solid color with three-quarter length sleeves made for action living. Sizes small, medium and large. Be "boss" by being first to own the new Bat-Men shirt-jacket. ONLY 11.95!

MAIL ORDERS FILLED PROMPTLY
CORNER BEALE AND SECOND STS.

88 | LANSKY BROTHERS: *CLOTHIER TO THE KING*

LEFT | Horsing Around

Elvis at Graceland in the 1960s wearing a houndstooth hat from Lansky Brothers (also below). Bernard often took Hal and his daughter Anise horseback riding at Graceland on Sunday mornings. "Most of the time Elvis wasn't there," Hal remembers, "but on a couple of occasions he was!"

ABOVE AND LEFT | Fashion Police

Elvis stops by a car accident to offer assistance in the mid 1970s, wearing the red leather Lansky Brothers coat shown at left.

THE KING'S NEW CLOTHES 89

Above: James Brown, with Bernard in the 1990s, was another famous Lansky customer.

the window at Lansky Brothers, the King of Rock 'n' Roll could buy racks and racks of clothes, shoes, and hats—and he loved to tell everyone where he got his stylish wardrobe.

Elvis quickly became the store's "goodwill ambassador," putting Lansky Brothers on the global map with his praise. "As Elvis spread the word," Bernard says, "calls from around the world began pouring in. Everyone wanted to dress like Elvis!"

Soon, "everyone" meant a long list of other well-known musicians that included Ace Cannon, B. B. King, David Porter, Bobby "Blue" Bland, Count Basie, the Beach Boys, Booker T. & the MGs, Charlie Rich, Lionel Hampton, Duke Ellington, Jerry Lee Lewis, the O'Jays, Isaac Hayes, Carl Perkins, the Temptations, Roy Orbison, and Otis Redding.

Elvis wasn't the store's only well-known PR representative, though. Blues recording artist Rufus Thomas, who hosted the amateur show at the Palace Theater where B. B. King and Bobby "Blue" Bland were discovered, was also effusive about Lansky's clothing. "For years," Bernard says, "Rufus would go on stage and show off his stylish cat clothes. He'd say, 'Ain't I clean? I got it at Lansky's!'"

to Bernard and asked him to find him the coat shown in the picture. A few moments later, Bernard returned with a formal morning coat from Lansky's tuxedo department. It was an exact match—and the beginning of Cash's legacy as the "Man in Black."

90 LANSKY BROTHERS: *CLOTHIER TO THE KING*

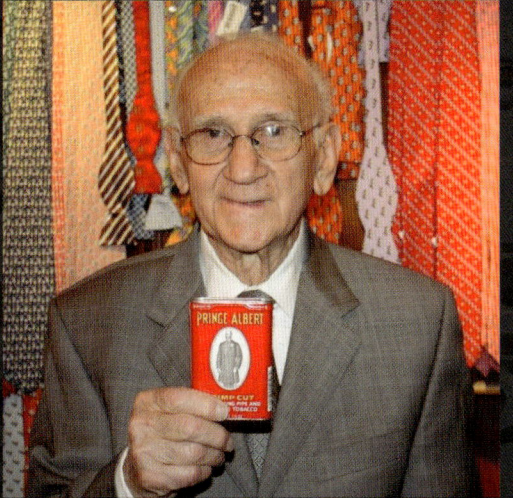

Elvis and blues musician Rufus Thomas were both longtime Lansky customers.

Above: Bernard holds the Prince Albert tobacco can that Johnny Cash brought into the store.

Elvis and Rufus Thomas preferred extravagant styles, but other customers, such as Johnny Cash, were more conservative. Bernard remembers that for Johnny Cash's first suit, he "brought me a Prince Albert tobacco can and pointed to the man on the cover. 'I want a black suit,' he said. So I made him a cutaway coat with black pants. Didn't have to worry about him—he always wore black."

Luckily for Lansky Brothers, its most famous customer—Elvis Aaron Presley—left a legacy of style that, even three decades later, is still as unique and memorable as the man himself.

Below: The stool that Elvis used while being fitted at Lansky Brothers now bears a plaque memorializing him.

ELVIS USED THIS FITTING PLATFORM MANY TIMES IN HIS CAREER.

HE STOOD TALL AND PROUD HERE. AS HE STANDS IN OUR MEMORY.

Elvis's closet, as seen here at Graceland in the 1970s, included a wide variety of colors and embellishments, both in his casual wear and stage costumes.

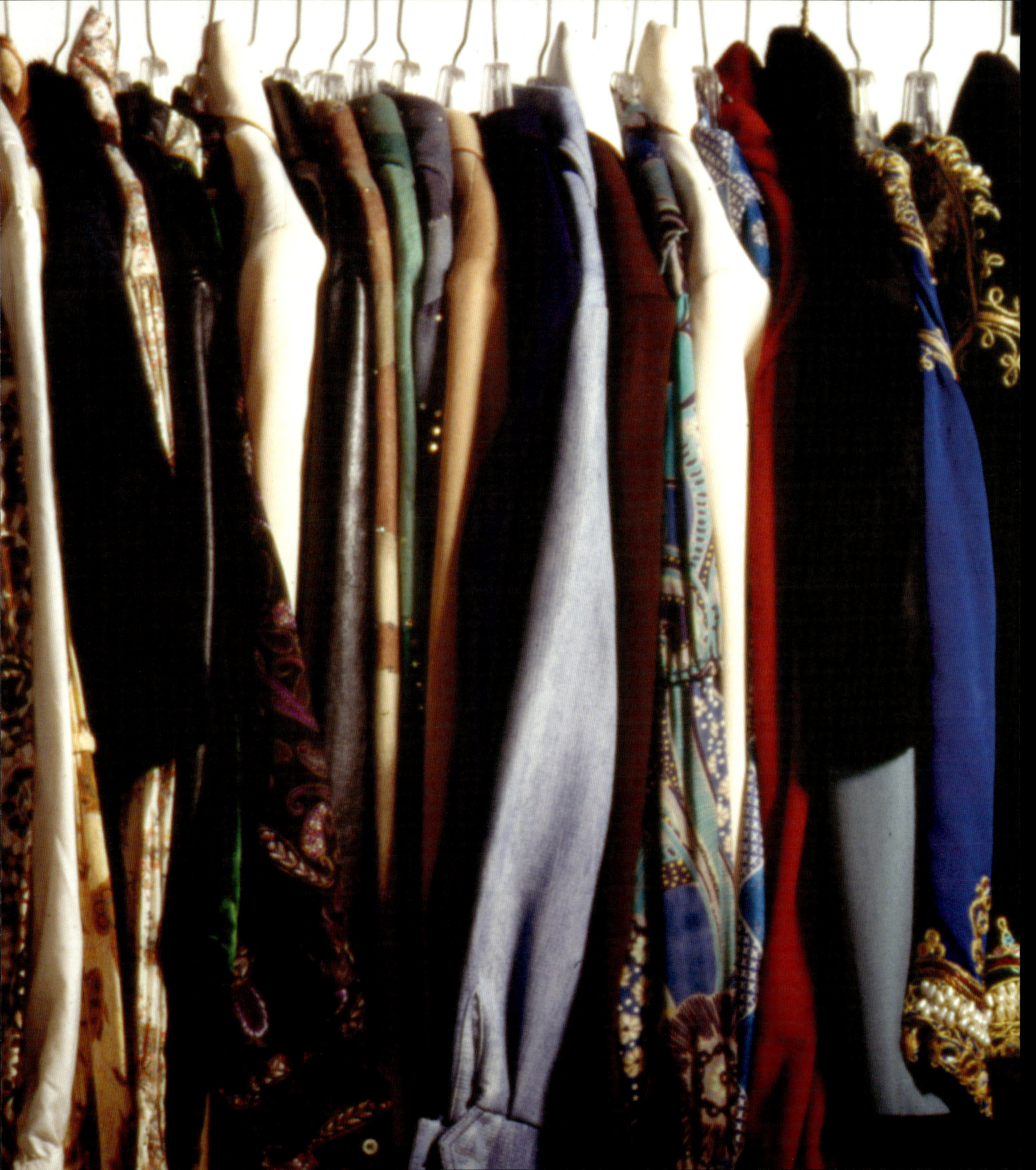

ABOVE AND LEFT | Custom Clothiers

Lansky Brothers created and custom tailored hundreds of shirts, jackets, and pants for Elvis Presley, including this white leather trench coat with black fur collar and cuffs (photographed at Graceland). All Elvis's custom clothing had the tags at left sewn inside.

LEFT | Fame and Fortune
Since the 1950s, Elvis loved buying scarves from Lansky Brothers, such as the white one here, to toss to his adoring fans while onstage.

BELOW | Denim Dragon
A Faded Glory dragon denim jacket from Lansky Brothers. The jacket has matching pants (not pictured) with a red glitter dragon going down the legs.

LEFT | Bells and Whistles
Another Lansky ad from the 1970s touted the store's "Tom Jones styling," with Captain Blood full-sleeved shirts and bell bottom pants—all "direct from the California coast."

RIGHT | Forget Me Never

Elvis waves to fans in the late 1970s. Touted as his "comeback" era, the seventies were a busy time for Elvis as he performed live from Las Vegas and toured in more than five hundred shows.

"He was a heck of a nice guy. I put him in his *first suit* and I put him in his *last suit*."
—Bernard Lansky

ABOVE AND LEFT | Man in Black

Elvis often wore this black and white fur coat—with matching black fur hat—from Lansky Brothers during his later years. The coat has black and white rabbit fur on the collar and cuffs, with white leather on the front panels and pockets.

96 LANSKY BROTHERS: *CLOTHIER TO THE KING*

Elvis pulls into the driveway at Graceland after a late-night doctor's appointment wearing the coat at left. This is reportedly the last-known photograph of the King of Rock 'n' Roll.

RIGHT AND BELOW | Good-Bye, Elvis

A portrait of Elvis taken in July 1970. Elvis Presley passed away on August 16, 1977. The next day, Bernard placed this full-page tribute below to his best customer and longtime friend in the Memphis Press-Scimitar. Fittingly, Elvis was buried in a white Lansky suit, light blue shirt, and white tie.

ELVIS.

...You were a man who touched the lives of so many....You were a star whom the world is poorer for the loss. ...You were gifted beyond belief. ...You were the man...the star...the king of the world of music.

It was just twenty-three years ago we first met you. We noticed you, staring into our shop windows, just looking...looking. You were so young,...friendly,...mannerly...and oh, so sure of your future. We became good friends, and for the rest of our lives we shall have the lasting memory of your friendship.

Bernard J. Lansky

LANSKY

"I was down in Dallas, in the markets, when we heard that Elvis had died. We flew right home—we knew that we had to do something. Right away, I went out to Graceland."
—Bernard Lansky

98   LANSKY BROTHERS: *CLOTHIER TO THE KING*

ABOVE | I'll Remember You

The passing of Elvis Presley left an enormous void in the music world and in the hearts of his adoring fans. Letters poured in from people who were touched by Bernard's tribute to Elvis. As Bernard says, "We all thought that he would be here forever. He was a heck of a nice guy."

THE KING'S NEW CLOTHES 99

This large mural on the side of the Lansky building on Beale Street was created by acclaimed local artist George Hunt in the 1970s. Hunt supervised the painting through CETA, a program that employed urban teens for summer jobs. The government paid more than $40,000 for the project.

LANSKY
FREE! CUSTOMERS PARKING
$2.00 Charge FOR ALL OTHERS
VIOLATORS CARS WILL BE TOWED
AWAY AT OWNERS EXPENSE
LANSKY MEN'S FASHIONS
DELTA

LANSKY BROTHERS: *CLOTHIER TO THE KING*

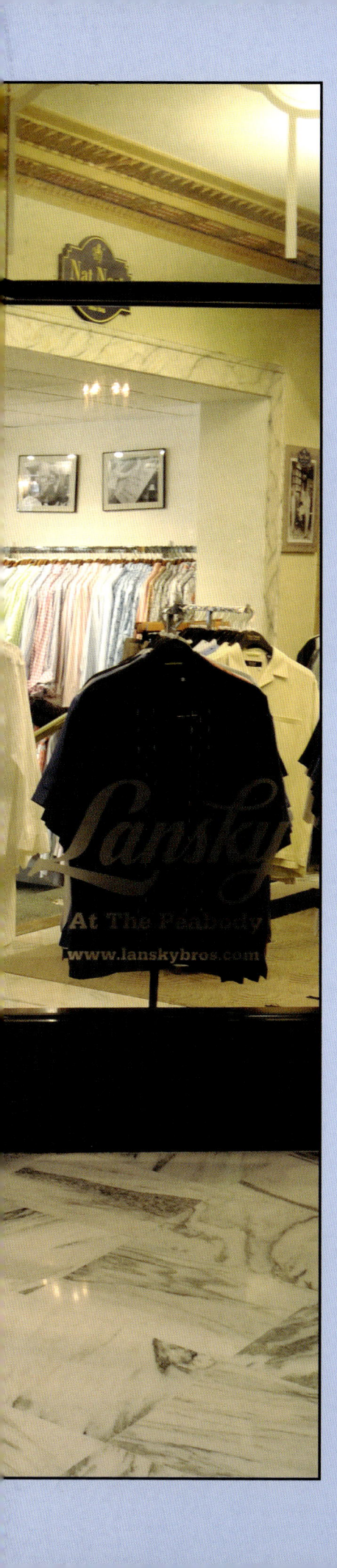

Part Three

THE LANSKY LEGACY

Late 1960s–Present

From the late 1960s to late 1970s, much of the United States experienced sweeping change—and downtown Memphis was no exception. After Martin Luther King Jr. was assassinated in 1968 on the balcony of Mulberry Street's Lorraine Motel, the area suffered from racially charged riots and crime. Soon nearby Beale Street—formerly a vibrant hub of music and culture—became a virtual ghost town, marked by dilapidated buildings and torn up pavement. "For years after the riots," remembers Hal Lansky, "there was a stigma that it was unsafe to go shopping downtown. It was like a war zone."

Fortunately for Bernard and Hal Lansky, while the store at 126 Beale Street was still the company's flagship location, they had also expanded to neighboring Whitehaven, East Memphis, and Raleigh.

LEFT | More in Store
Lansky at the Peabody opens to the marbled interior of the Peabody hotel and has windows looking outside to Union Avenue, giving the store a spacious feel.

Above | Steadfast, Loyal, and True

As their only surviving child, Elvis was extremely close to his parents. His father, Vernon, was devastated when his son passed away in 1977; Vernon died of heart failure just two years later.

The Whitehaven store was near Graceland, and Vernon Presley dropped by frequently to shop. "We were always busy," recalls Hal, "working around the clock to stock all our stores with the most upscale, fashionable clothes."

Other local businesses did not fare as well. In the mid-1970s, after more than one hundred years in business, the historic Peabody hotel went bankrupt. To save it from being turned into a parking lot, Lansky family friend and developer Jack Belz purchased the Peabody in 1975 for $400,000 and took it through a six-year, $25 million renovation. Bernard opened a tie shop in the newly reconstructed hotel as a favor to Mr. Belz. This small specialty store, called Peabody Ltd., opened in 1981 and would later be one of several shops that would make up the core of the business.

The move was typical of the Lanskys. "We always wanted to change things up to adapt to the times," says Hal. In 1980, Bernard bought out his brother Guy's interest in the company, and Bernard became CEO and Hal was named president. Under their leadership, the Lansky brand changed focus again. For years the stores had carried "Big and Tall" sizes along with their regular merchandise. These large sizes soon started to outsell their other clothing, so in the mid-1980s, the Lanskys decided to change their business to exclusively Big and Tall apparel. "We were everything to everybody and nothing to nobody," explains Hal. "We needed to specialize." It was a risk. Lansky's accountants advised against the move; at the time, Lansky's regular-size clothing business made up 60 percent of the company's inventory—and revenue. But there was virtually no competition in the big and tall industry, and soon the new business soared. The Lanskys' Big and Tall stores of the Mid-South expanded to nine locations. In 1994, they were sold at a substantial profit.

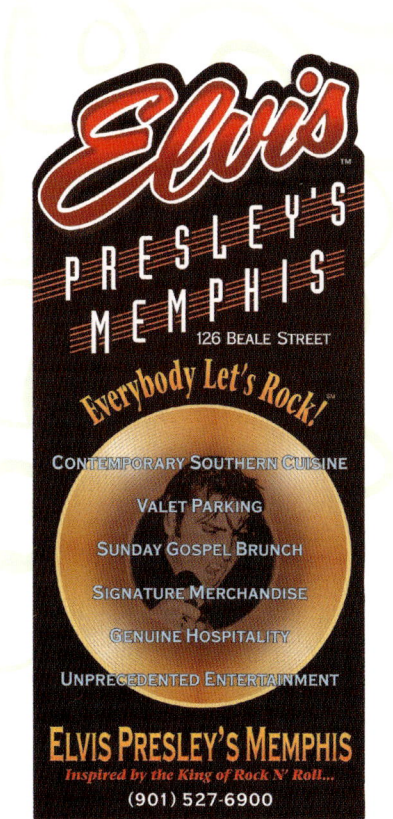

ABOVE | It's in the Cards
A 1997 marketing card for Elvis Presley's Memphis, a nightclub and restaurant established by the King's estate in the late 1990s. The restaurant—located in the Lansky building at 126 Beale Street—featured Southern cooking, entertainment, and Elvis merchandise.

Sales at 126 Beale, however, suffered. Over time, the street had become more known for its entertainment venues than retail stores. Hal and Bernard closed the original location in 1992, using it as an office and a warehouse for its various suburban locations. In 1996, Elvis Presley Enterprises signed a twenty-year lease with the Lanskys to renovate the space and build "Elvis Presley's Memphis," a restaurant and club that specialized in Southern cooking, including Elvis's favorite fried peanut butter and banana sandwiches. The eatery opened in August 1997, on the twentieth anniversary of Elvis's death, to booming business. Unfortunately, the restaurant could not sustain the popularity of its early years. After the terrorist attacks on September 11, 2001, the tourism industry dwindled, and many themed restaurants suffered. Elvis Presley's Memphis—in many ways a destination site—closed in 2003.

Fortunately, the Peabody was another matter. The restoration of the historic hotel had slowly revitalized the area, and sales at Peabody Ltd. were brisk. In 1994, after selling the Big and Tall stores, Hal and Bernard changed the name of their small boutique to Lansky at the Peabody. Like its predecessor on Beale Street, Lansky at the Peabody carries fashionable menswear, including limited edition merchandise not found in traditional department stores.

Hal and Bernard expanded their Peabody operations as other space in the hotel became available. In 1996, they opened Lansky Essentials, which sells magazines, toiletries, and incidentals. That year they also took over the space that sold merchandise related to the Peabody's famous ducks, and changed the name to Lansky Lucky Duck. They operated another gift store, the Lansky Logo Shop, as well. After just eighteen months, though, they closed the logo shop to make room for a newer, more profitable venture: Lansky 126.

ABOVE | A Big Deal
An ad from the 1960s featured a January sale on Lansky Big and Tall merchandise, including stadium, corduroy leisure, and clicker coats.

THE LANSKY LEGACY   105

The Lansky shops all stretch out along the front of the Peabody on Union Avenue.

106   LANSKY BROTHERS: *CLOTHIER TO THE KING*

BELOW | The Tin Man
This large tin cut-out hung outside Lansky Brothers for many years, advertising the store's formal wear rentals.

Unlike Lansky at the Peabody, Lansky 126 carries women's as well as men's clothing. The idea for the store began when Hal noticed the trend in designer denim taking place around the country. Hal and Bernard were eager to expand their customer base—and when Hal's daughter Julie joined the company in 2002, she helped to reach these younger customers by introducing new merchandising techniques, launching a strong Web presence, and bringing the latest trends to Memphis. "You have to get in there and experiment," explains Hal. "It's the only way to stay relevant." The store caters to a younger demographic and features casual designer clothing. Yet it is not such a departure from the original store on Beale Street, where Elvis Presley began shopping as a teenager. "Hopefully, like my grandfather did with Elvis, we can draw younger people to 126 and retain them as loyal customers," Julie says.

The Lanskys are planning for more growth, particularly in the areas of franchising, international expansion, and Web sales. But while the brand has experienced decades of change—from army surplus to cat clothes to menswear to casual women's clothing—one thing remains constant: The Lansky name continues to represent quality merchandise that "has a little something extra," Bernard says.

This uniqueness, of course, is what first piqued the interest of the King of Rock 'n' Roll. More than anyone, it was Bernard Lansky who helped shape Elvis's style. Now in his eighties and still working full time, Bernard likes to pronounce a blessing of sorts over his customers. "May we all have the style of Elvis," he tells them. With an eye on the future and strong roots in the past, the Lanskys are helping people all over the world to do just that.

ABOVE | Pomp and Circumstance
Elvis in the 1960s, sporting a pompadour and a stylish green jacket with black lacing up the sleeves and pockets.

THE LANSKY LEGACY   107

ABOVE | Reaching Great Heights

Bernard helps a customer inside one of his Big and Tall stores. The Lansky Big and Tall stores of the Mid-South were a huge success, eventually growing to nine stores. In 1994, the Lanskys sold the chain for a substantial profit.

"We were *everything to everybody and nothing to nobody.* We needed to specialize in *Big and Tall Sizes.*"
—Hal Lansky

ABOVE | Gift Guide

In the mid-1960s, Lansky Brothers began focusing on its Big and Tall merchandise. This 1965 holiday advertisement for the Beale Street store told customers looking for larger sizes, "Your worries are over. Lansky Brothers has . . . everything you could wish for."

108 LANSKY BROTHERS: *CLOTHIER TO THE KING*

A late 1970s picture of the Lansky Brothers outpost in Raleigh, Tennessee, a suburb of Memphis.

Soul musicians and songwriting team Isaac Hayes (left) and David Porter (right) shop for clothes with a Lansky Brothers employee in the late 1960s. That decade, Hayes and Porter penned more than two hundred songs for Memphis-based label Stax Records. They were inducted into the Songwriting Hall of Fame in 2005.

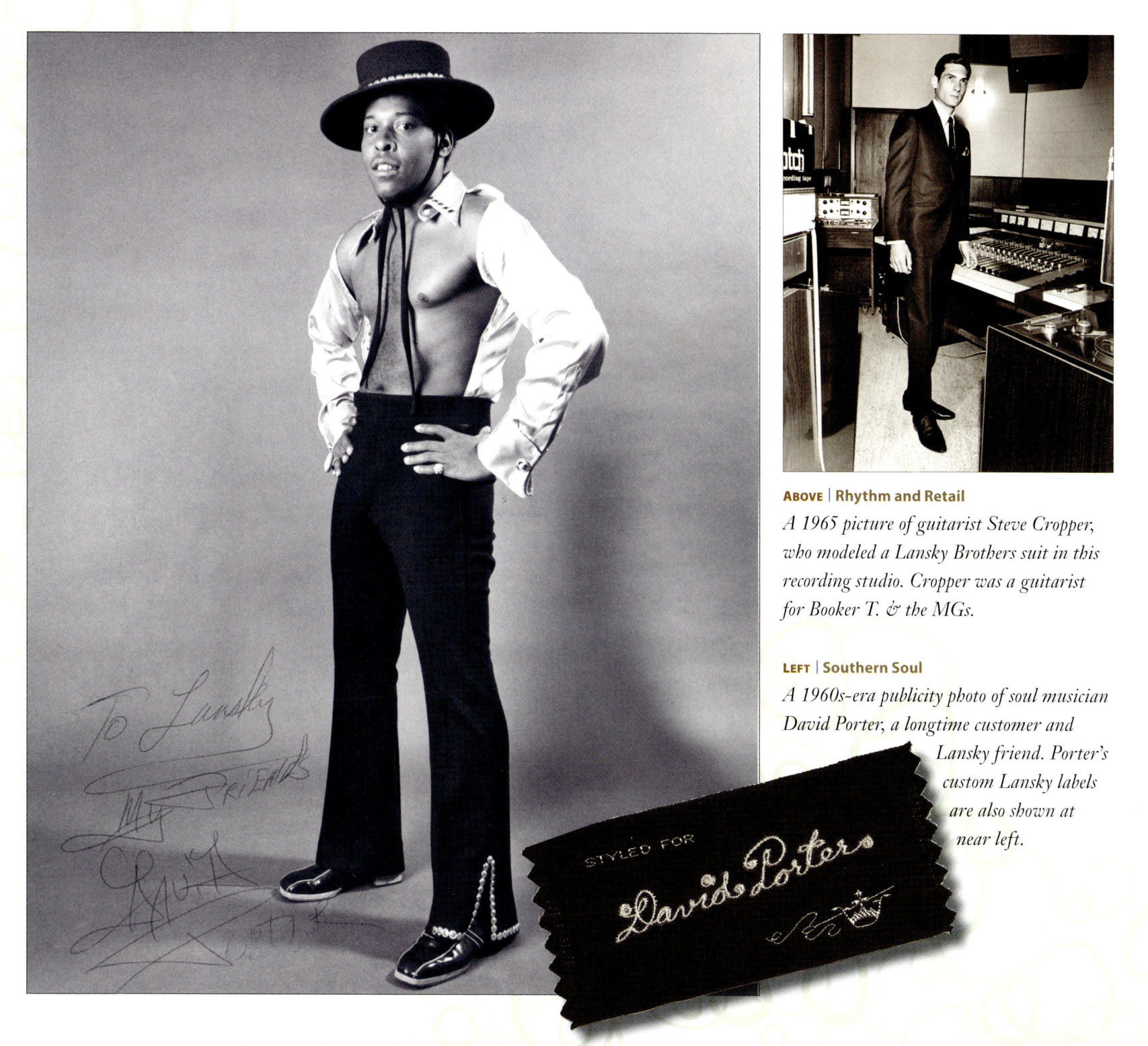

ABOVE | Rhythm and Retail
A 1965 picture of guitarist Steve Cropper, who modeled a Lansky Brothers suit in this recording studio. Cropper was a guitarist for Booker T. & the MGs.

LEFT | Southern Soul
A 1960s-era publicity photo of soul musician David Porter, a longtime customer and Lansky friend. Porter's custom Lansky labels are also shown at near left.

"If you ask for the pivotal points in my life and career, I would give them to you in this order: God, family, meeting Isaac Hayes, and the generosity shared to me as a young person by one Bernard Lansky. The beauty of the man is camouflaged quite often by the words and energy that he uses to finalize the sale! In truth, he is one of the most generous, kind, loyal, and intelligent people that anyone could meet."
— David Porter

THE LANSKY LEGACY   111

The Whitehaven storefront in the late 1960s featured a wide variety of suits and ties. The store was located close to Graceland, and both Elvis and his father, Vernon, often popped in to shop.

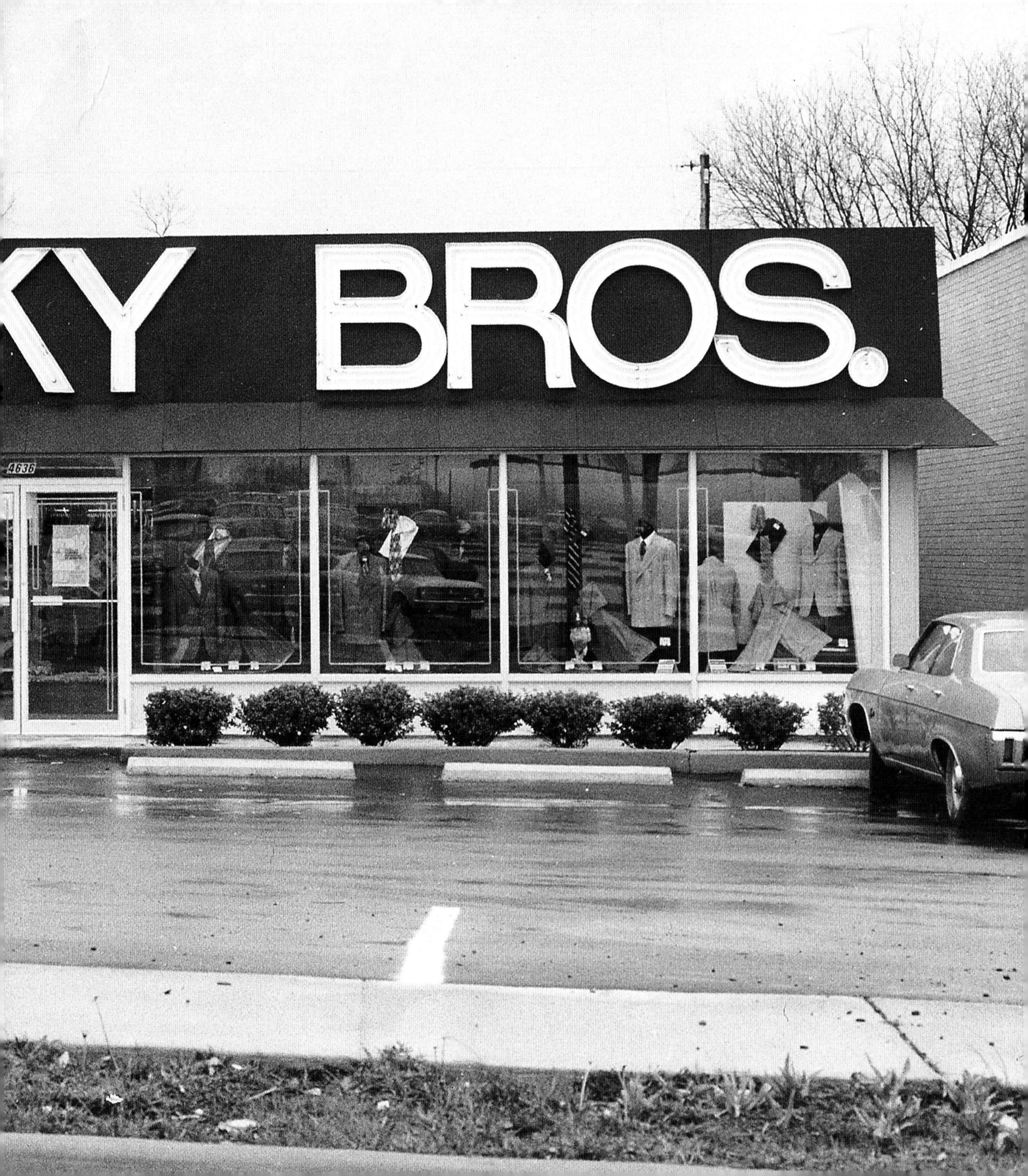
KY BROS.
4636

RIGHT | Grand "Sham" Style
Bernard and Grammy Award–winning rock 'n' roll artist Sam the Sham at Lansky Brothers. Sam the Sham, wearing a white rabbit fur coat, was a regular customer in the 1960s and 1970s.

BELOW RIGHT | Label Lover
Lansky Brothers created this label for Sam the Sham's custom clothing.

*"Lansky's the name,
　Fashion's the game.
　　You want it?
　　　He's got it.
　If he ain't got it,
　　He'll find it.
　If he caint find it,
　　You describe it and he'll make it.
　　　You won't have to fake it.
　　I know whereof I speak.
　It was on Beale where I got my deal.
　Go on with yourself, Bernard."*
　　　　　—Sam the Sham

114　LANSKY BROTHERS: *CLOTHIER TO THE KING*

ABOVE | The Superfly Seventies
Inside Lansky Brothers in the 1970s. The store carried the pimp hats, large sunglasses, and long leather coats pictured here that were stylish during the disco era.

LEFT | Lansky Labels
A roll of vintage sparkly clothing labels from the late 1950s.

THE LANSKY LEGACY

Bernard —
I'm still wearing your clothes!!
God bless ya
Pat Boone

OPPOSITE AND LEFT | **"Booning" Business**

An autographed picture of 1950s teen idol and longtime customer Pat Boone with Bernard at Lansky Brothers, and then fifty years later at left. Pat Boone is signing a dress shoe for display in the store.

BELOW | **It's in the Bag**

A vintage bag from Lansky Brothers on "Famous Beale Street."

LEFT | **I Get Around**

Bernard poses with several members of the Beach Boys and singer-songwriter Bobby Goldsboro (third from right) in Lansky Brothers in the 1960s.

THE LANSKY LEGACY 117

RIGHT | Local Legend
Danny Thomas, founder of St. Jude Children's Hospital in Memphis, stands in front of the original Lansky Brothers store in the early 1960s.

BELOW | Getting Labeled
For years, Lansky Brothers created custom labels for high profile clients like blues singers Bobby Bland and Albert King, and musician and WWE Hall of Fame Superstar Jimmy Hart.

118 LANSKY BROTHERS: *CLOTHIER TO THE KING*

ABOVE | Record Looks

Willie Mitchell (front left) and his band wear fashion-forward Nehru-collar jackets inside Lansky Brothers in the late 1960s. Mitchell, the famous producer and songwriter responsible for discovering Al Green, made some of the most successful soul albums of the time.

THE LANSKY LEGACY

The Peabody stood on the corner of Main Street and Monroe for more than five decades, before it was rebuilt on Union Avenue in the 1920s as shown here. The hotel was originally going to be named after its builder, Colonel Robert C. Brinkley, but Brinkley changed his mind right before the grand opening, when he learned that his good friend George Peabody had passed away.

THE PEABODY
1869–Present

Established in 1869 on the heels of the Civil War, the Peabody is one of downtown Memphis's main attractions. The original building—located on Main Street and Monroe—was once considered the premier institution of the "New South," playing host to czars, presidents, celebrities, and Southerners such as Robert E. Lee and Andrew Jackson. In 1923, it was demolished and rebuilt to more modern standards on the corner of Second and Union, where it still stands today.

The famous tradition of the Peabody ducks began at this site in 1932, when the general manager of the hotel and his hunting buddy decided to play a prank on hotel guests by putting three live duck decoys in the lobby's fountain. The guests and staff were delighted, and soon after the Peabody permanently housed five Northern American mallards. Then in 1940, hotel bellman and former circus trainer Edward Pembroke took things further by teaching the ducks to march from their home on the roof of the hotel to the lobby below. This spectacle continues today as the ducks—led by a duckmaster—make their way to the marble fountain at 11:00 each morning.

Yet even the famous ducks couldn't sustain the Peabody after the assassination of Martin Luther King Jr. in 1968. Downtown Memphis went into severe economic decline, and the Peabody was shuttered in the 1970s, unable to overcome the stigma of its location. In 1975, Belz Enterprises purchased the hotel and took it through an extensive renovation. It reopened in 1981, featuring a new Lansky shop, Peabody Ltd., the first of several Lansky stores that would operate in the hotel. Now called Lansky at the Peabody, this formerly small store—and its younger counterpart, Lansky 126—has become as much a part of the hotel's identity as its legendary Southern hospitality and storied past.

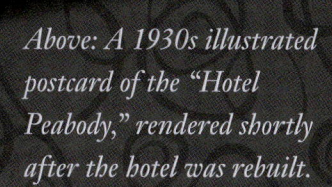

Above: The famous fountain in the lobby of the Peabody, circa 1925. Author and historian David Cohn once wrote of the Peabody, "If you stand near its fountain in the middle of the lobby . . . ultimately you will see everybody who is anybody in the Delta."

Above: A 1930s illustrated postcard of the "Hotel Peabody," rendered shortly after the hotel was rebuilt.

THE LANSKY LEGACY   121

RIGHT | Rock 'n' Royal Blue

Led Zeppelin lead singer Robert Plant with Bernard at Lansky at the Peabody in 2009.

BELOW | Guitar Heroes

More than seventy guitars—autographed by music legends such as Elvis Presley, Johnny Cash, Robert Plant, Billy Joel, and James Taylor—line the eighteen-foot walls inside Lansky at the Peabody.

"He [Bernard] threw fabric, style, and color onto the shoulders of the whirlwind—together, they saved us from the grey."

—Robert Plant, lead singer of Led Zeppelin

122 LANSKY BROTHERS: *CLOTHIER TO THE KING*

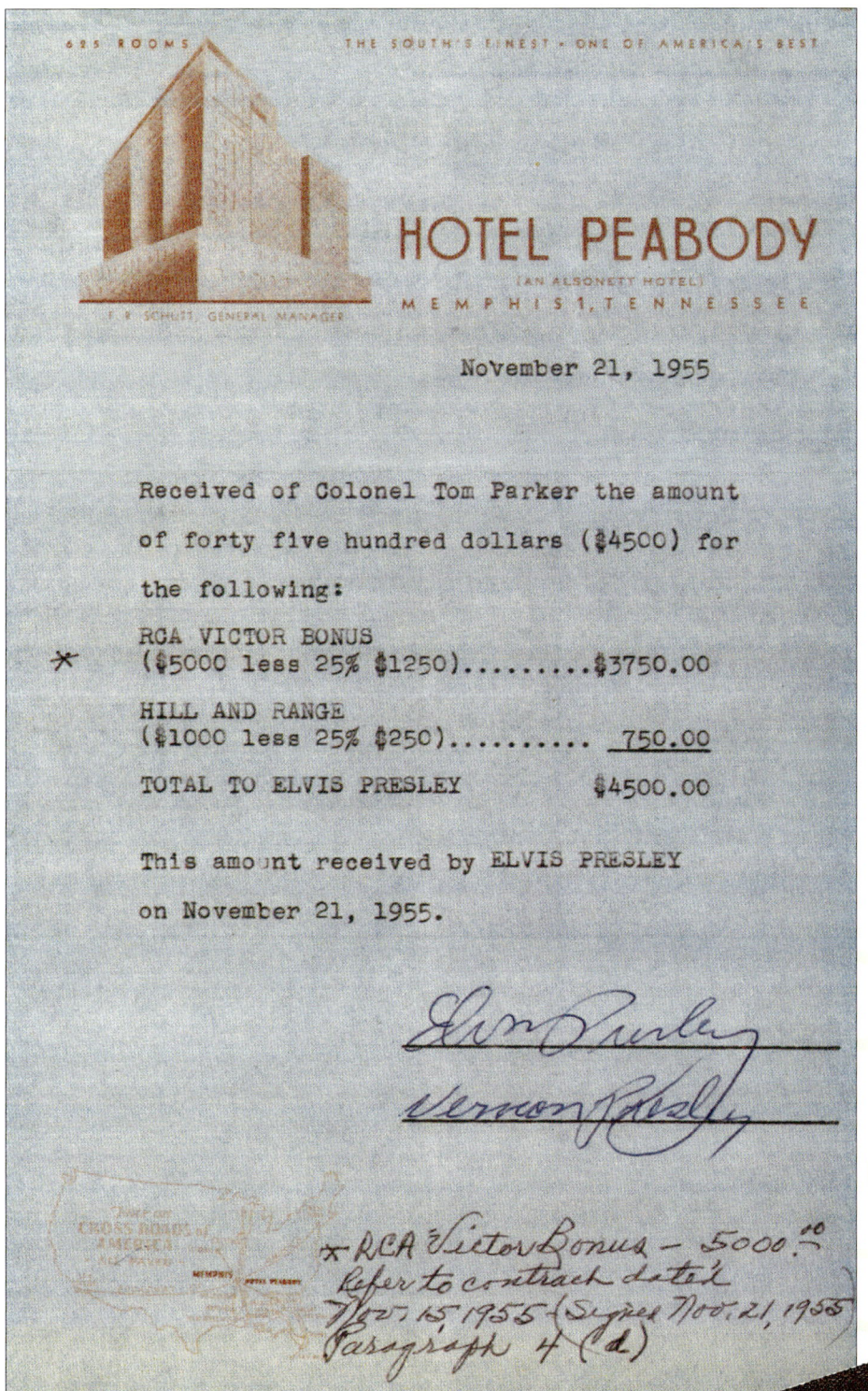

ABOVE | Famous Flip
Bernard Lansky flips the collar of best-selling recording artist Chris Isaak.

BELOW | Peabody Pride
These labels are sewn into the clothes sold at Lansky at the Peabody.

"You never know who will walk into our doors!"
—Bernard Lansky

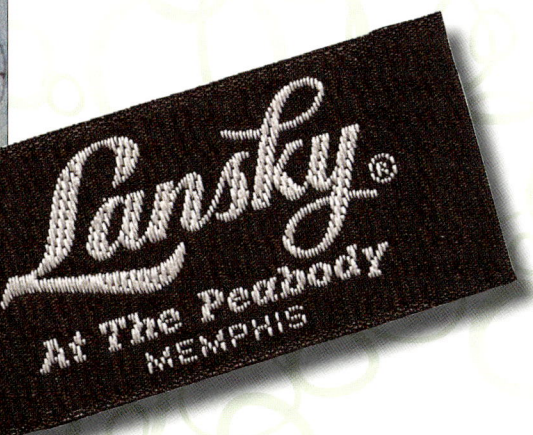

ABOVE | Signed, Sealed, and Delivered
In 1999, Elvis again made headlines when a receipt that he and his father, Vernon Presley, signed on stationery from the historic Peabody hotel was sold for $65,000. Elvis's manager, Colonel Parker, had been staying at the Peabody and had the receipt typed up on the hotel stationery. Dated 1955, it marked the beginning of Elvis's recording career with RCA.

THE LANSKY LEGACY   123

Inside Lansky at the Peabody, Bernard Lansky (far left) works the counter—and the crowd.

LEFT | Pink Mink
Elvis sent this fur-trimmed pink leather coat to Lansky Brothers for repair shortly before he died in 1977. He never picked it up. Today it is on display inside Lansky at the Peabody.

BELOW LEFT | Banding Together
Fanny Alger, a music group from Washington, wears Speedway jackets from Lansky's line, Clothier to the King.

BELOW | Shear Genius
A pair of scissors from the original store on Beale Street.

"It's amazing how many international customers come through our doors. They might not be able to speak English, but they know all of Elvis's songs by heart!"
—Hal Lansky

THE LANSKY LEGACY 125

More than sixty years later, Bernard Lansky still works at the store seven days a week, eight to twelve hours a day. His son Hal says, "We're both at the store more than we are at home!"

LANSKY AT THE PEABODY

1981–Present

Memphis is known for its rich music history—and its most famous menswear store, Lansky at the Peabody, has been giving customers a front-row education in rhythm, blues, and style since 1946. Inside the opulent lobby of the Peabody hotel, this upscale, 1,800-square-foot store is covered from floor to ceiling with guitars signed by country, pop, and rock 'n' roll stars such as Elvis Presley, Billy Joel, James Taylor, and Van Morrison. The most famous of these, of course, is Elvis, whose clothing eventually became as legendary as his music. Elvis was Bernard Lansky's most loyal customer from his teenage years until his death in 1977, and artifacts and memorabilia from that time period line the store's eighteen-foot walls. There are images of Bernard styling the King, and the pink fur jacket Elvis wore during his superfly days is prominently on display.

Elvis was drawn to the original shop on Beale Street for its unique, extravagant style. Today, Bernard, his son Hal, and his granddaughter Julie are keeping this legacy alive through their line Clothier to the King. Created in connection with the King's estate, the collection offers Elvis-inspired pieces from the 1950s and 60s. "The kids want the vintage look, and that's what we've got," says Bernard. "It's old to us, but new to them." The private label—launched on the twenty-fifth anniversary of Elvis's death—features retro shirts, pants, and jackets in shiny silks, leathers, and velvets, along with items in the pink and black palate that Bernard helped Elvis to make famous in the 1950s. The store also carries a variety of other popular brands, including Nat Nast, Robert Graham, Tulliano, Cole Haan, Hiltl, Agave Denim, Donald Pliner, Bugatchi, Thomas Dean, Hush Puppies, and Ike Behar. "When we buy for this store," says Hal, "we purchase the icing on the cake."

Below: Pink and black, the color combination that Bernard Lansky made famous in the 1950s, is still as popular as ever. Pictured are several shirts from Lansky's clothing line, Clothier to the King.

Above: A Lansky advertisement features this "Walkin' in Memphis" shirt, based on the hit song by Grammy Award-winning singer-songwriter Marc Cohn.

THE LANSKY LEGACY 127

RIGHT | Orchestrated Style
Bernard Lansky with Brian Setzer, the frontman for Brian Setzer Orchestra, a popular jump, jive, and wail swing band.

OPPOSITE | Red Carpet Treatment
Each day at eleven o'clock, the famous Peabody ducks make their way to the lobby of the hotel, parading up a red carpet to splash in the fountain. They return to their home promptly at five o'clock.

RIGHT | I Met Her Today
The twentieth anniversary of Elvis's death in 1997 brought thousands of people to Memphis, including Katie Couric, who interviewed Bernard for the Today show.

"We're not in the retail business; we're in the tourism business."
—Hal and Julie Lansky

128 LANSKY BROTHERS: *CLOTHIER TO THE KING*

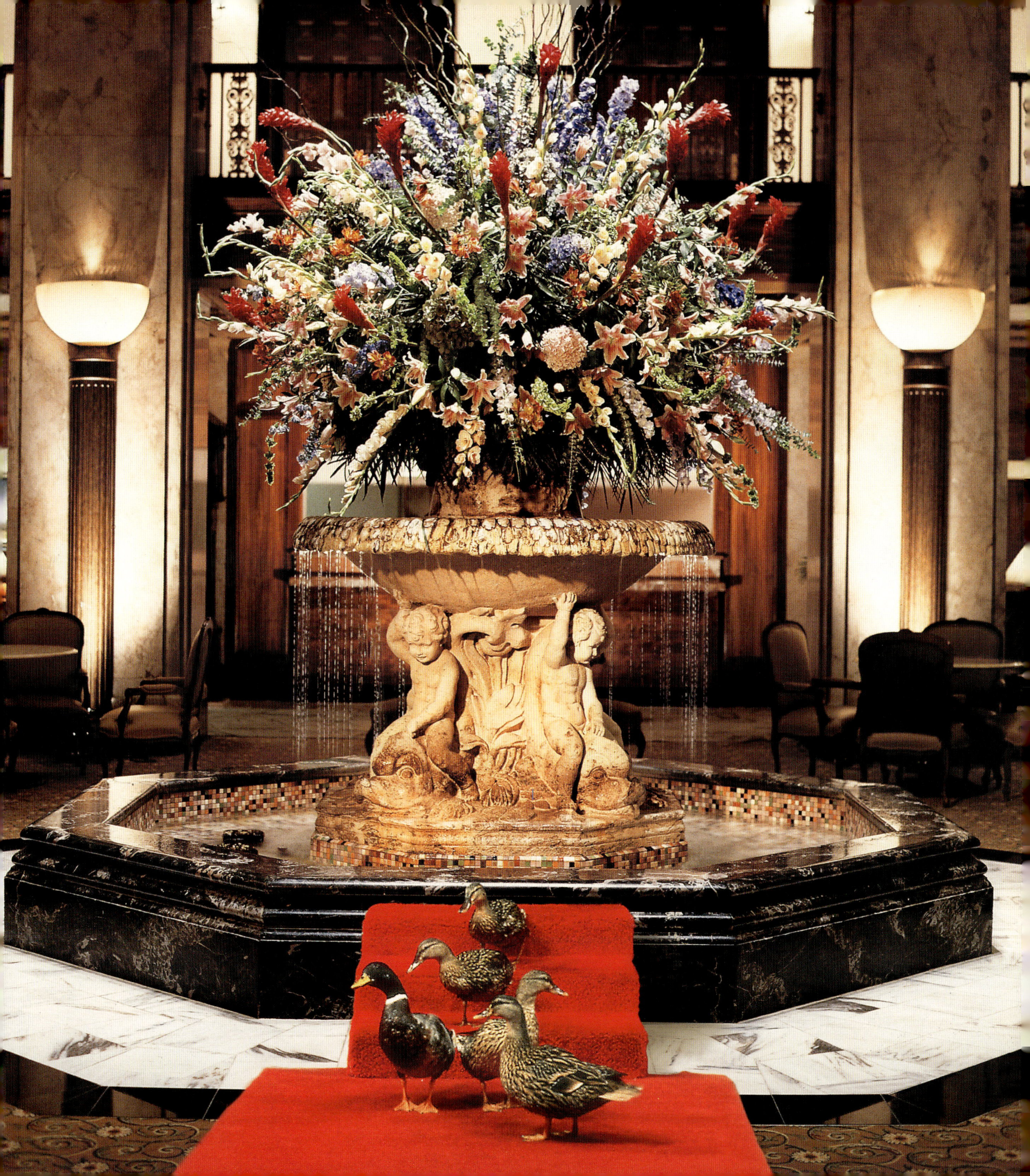

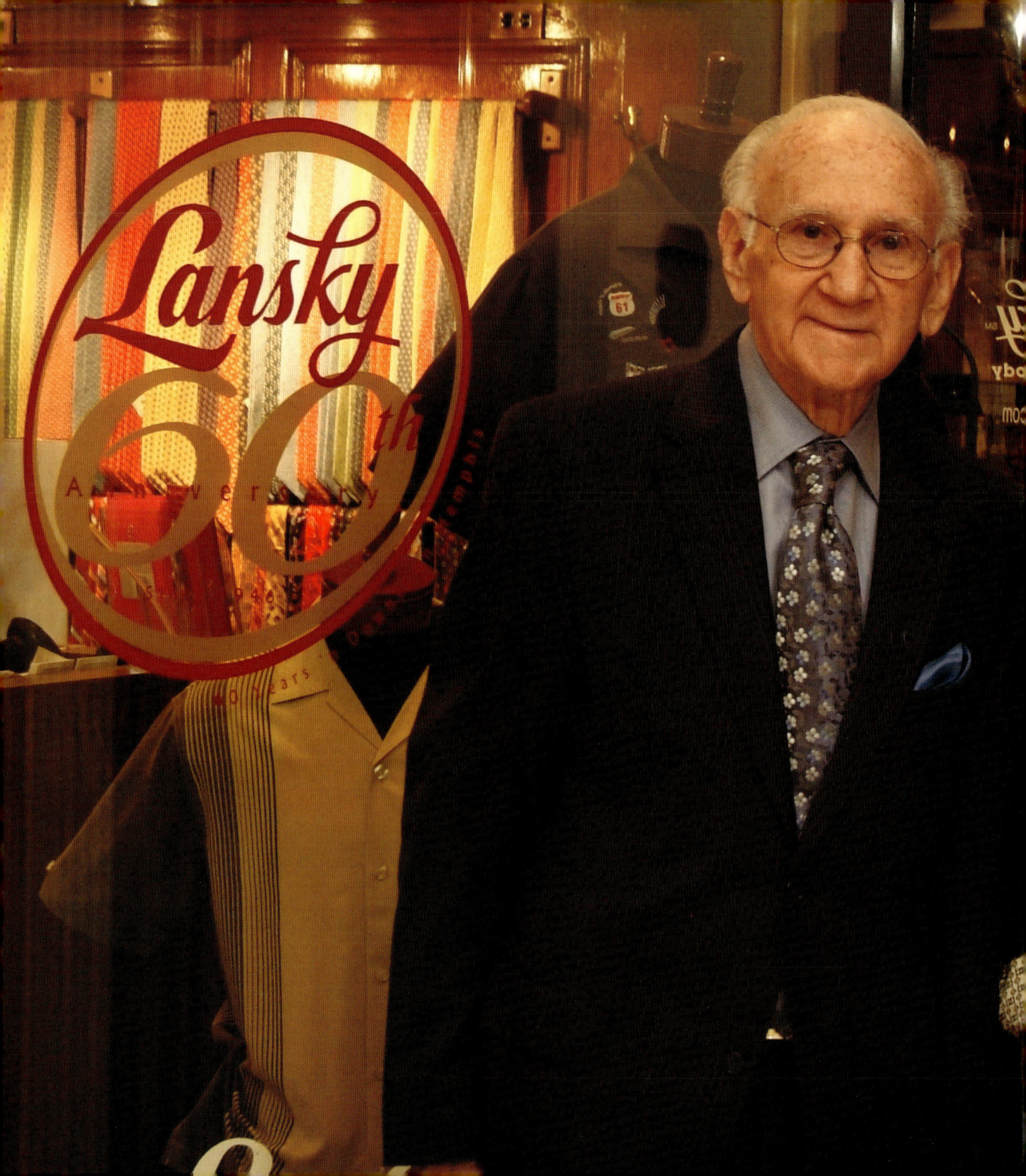
Lansky
60th

Bernard, Julie, and Hal Lansky celebrate Lansky's "Sixty Years in Downtown Memphis" in 2006.

Looking Ahead with Lansky 126

2003–Present

"We sell sizzle," Hal and Julie Lansky like to say, and nowhere is that more evident than at the company's newest store, Lansky 126. Located next to Lansky at the Peabody, Lansky 126 carries the latest styles and accessories for young men and women, including men's sport shirts, denim, tees, sweaters, jackets, and accessories (jewelry, handbags, and shoes). Here, customers can find upscale brands—such as 7 for All Mankind, True Religion Brand Jeans, Lacoste, Diesel, 7 Diamonds, BCBG, Michael Stars, UGG Australia—as well as friendly staff members to help them locate that perfectly fitting pair of jeans.

Julie Lansky, Hal's daughter, is the driving force behind the store. She joined the company soon after graduating from the University of Colorado-Boulder in 2001, originally to help relaunch and improve Lansky's Web presence. As she learned more about Lansky's younger, more contemporary customer base, she became increasingly involved in the store's operations. Today, Julie serves as the exclusive buyer for Lansky 126, stocking hard-to-find designer brands and trends seen in both New York and Los Angeles.

The idea for Lansky 126 began when Hal noticed an emerging trend in contemporary clothing and premium denim in some of the country's top markets. Hal and Bernard were eager to branch out from their menswear roots, so in 2003, they closed one of their underperforming gift shops and launched

Above: Julie Lansky and her grandfather Bernard don hats from Lansky 126.

Above: The logo for Lansky 126 bears the motto "Clothes That Rock."

Lansky 126. The experiment paid off. Lansky 126—named after the original store on Beale Street—has already expanded several times, more than doubling in size from 800 to 2,700 square feet. Celebrity clients include musicians Keith Urban, Jason Mraz, and Sheryl Crow; actor and racecar driver Danica Patrick; the band Live; and actors Angela Bassett and John Corbitt.

"When trends evolve," says Julie, "I get excited to see what's new. But then I'm reminded of what my grandfather always says: 'What goes around comes around.' When you've been in the business for more than sixty-five years, you know that nothing is really new. The designers have just put a modern spin on it." Just like the Lanskys have done with their latest store.

Above: Julie Lansky helped develop a more strategic merchandising plan for Lansky 126. "Now our denim is featured by brand," says Julie, "instead of having everything folded into the walls."

THE LANSKY LEGACY 133

Bernard Lansky and Priscilla Presley gather in the lobby of the Peabody hotel to celebrate Elvis's 2007 induction into the Peabody Duck Walk Hall of Fame. Elvis attended his senior prom at the Peabody hotel in the mid-1950s—wearing a Lansky tuxedo.

LEFT | Home from Hollywood
Nicolas Cage visits Hal and Bernard at Lansky at the Peabody in 2002.

LEFT | Having a Ball
Bernard and Hal Lansky with Dennis Quaid, in character as Jerry Lee Lewis on the set of his 1989 movie Great Balls of Fire! *The movie recreated the Lansky Brothers store (seen here) as it appeared in the 1950s.*

"When Elvis fans come to Memphis, they want to go to Lansky's. They want to shop where Elvis shopped!"
—Bernard Lansky

THE LANSKY LEGACY

Inside Lansky at the Peabody. The store sells high end menswear, including merchandise from Nat Nast, Robert Graham, Tulliano, Bugatchi, Thomas Dean, and its own line, Clothier to the King.

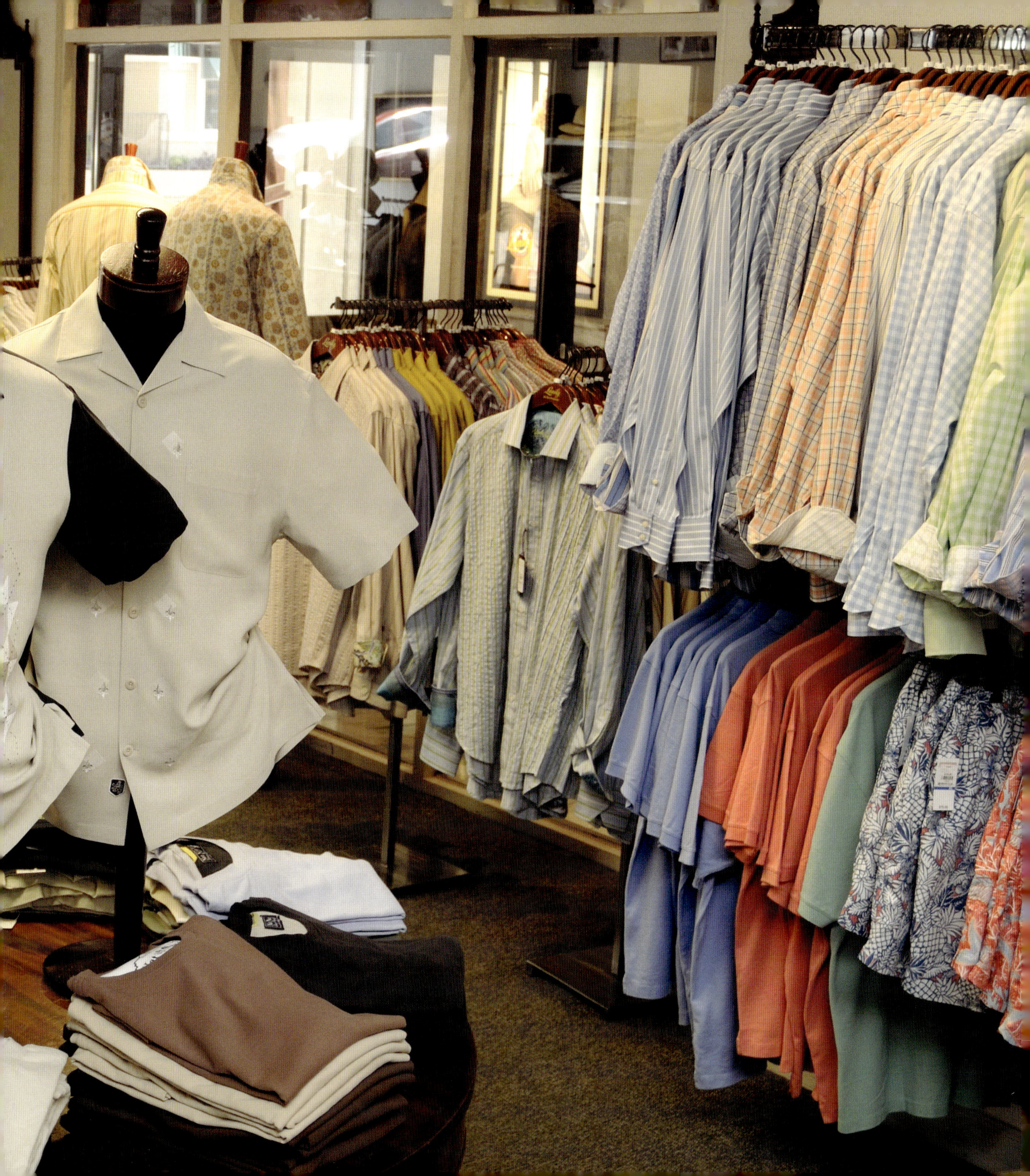

RIGHT | News and Neckties

Larry King sent Bernard a thank you note after receiving a tie from Lansky's Clothier to the King collection.

BELOW | A Little Less Conversation

Bernard Lansky presents cable giant Larry King with a "Love Me Tender" necktie during a 2007 duck walk at the Peabody hotel.

CNN — LARRY KING

Dear Bernard,

Thank you for the "Love Me Tender" tie from your shop. I will think of you and your amazing career with "The King" when I wear it. I will never forget your generosity to this Brooklyn guy!

Best wishes,

LEFT | Nothin' but a Groundhog
Actor Bill Murray, who appeared in Groundhog Day *and* Lost in Translation, *with Bernard Lansky circa 2007.*

BELOW | Love Me Tender
This black velvet blousy "Love Me Tender" shirt is similar to one Gladys Presley made for Elvis to wear during his Tupelo Fairgrounds concert in 1956. It was recreated as part of the Clothier to the King collection on the twenty-fifth anniversary of Elvis's death.

LEFT | Girl of Mine
Linda Thompson, a former Miss Tennessee who dated Elvis Presley from 1972 to 1976, visits Bernard at the store during the thirtieth anniversary of Elvis Week in 2007.

THE LANSKY LEGACY

A Rock 'n' Roll Legacy

Since 1946

"We're not in the retail business," the Lanskys often say. "We're in the tourism business." And their dozens of celebrity clients can testify to that. Drawn by the heritage of the Lansky name and the quality it promises, entertainers from every background—from sports to television to music to movies—visit the Lansky stores to be dressed by the family that was clothier to the King. Their images adorn the walls of Lansky at the Peabody and Lansky 126, and include Billy Bob Thornton, Katie Couric, Robert Plant, Jimmy Page, Steven Tyler, Nicolas Cage, Lisa Marie Presley, Robin Williams, Uncle Kracker, Carrie Underwood, Richard Simmons, Jonathan Rhys-Meyers, Linda Evans, Chris Isaak, Pat Boone, and Lynard Skynard.

The Lansky family and staff have outfitted rock royalty ever since Bernard Lansky began stocking the first "cat clothes" of the 1950s. Many of the artists come to buy clothes and then stay to talk. Bernard recalls the time in which Sheryl Crow visited the store and mentioned that she needed a ride to the airport. "I drove her there in my Buick Roadmaster wagon," he says. Another time Robert Plant and Jimmy Page of Led Zeppelin were in town for a concert and stopped by. "They were real nice guys," remembers Bernard. "As a matter of fact, they invited me to their show."

Below: Inside Lansky 126 with Julie Lansky and Johnny Rotten, lead singer of the British punk group the Sex Pistols.

Above: Grammy Award-winning singer-songwriter Sheryl Crow visits with Bernard in 2001.

David Porter, a best-selling soul musician known for his popular collaborations in the 1960s with Isaac Hayes, has been a customer of the Lanskys for more than fifty years. Like Elvis, Porter was poor and needed help when starting out in the business. He explains: "I had no stage clothes and very few school clothes. In high school, I went to Lansky Brothers and spoke to both Bernard and his beautiful wife, asking if they would allow me to purchase a suit on credit. I promised that at some point in the future, I would pay them back. They let me have the suit with a spirit of generosity that has never been equaled in my life. I paid them back years later and have been buying from them ever since. I love the Lanskys!"

Above: Joe Perry, lead guitarist of Aerosmith, with Bernard in Lansky at the Peabody.

Left: Bernard Lansky with Robin Williams, circa 2005.

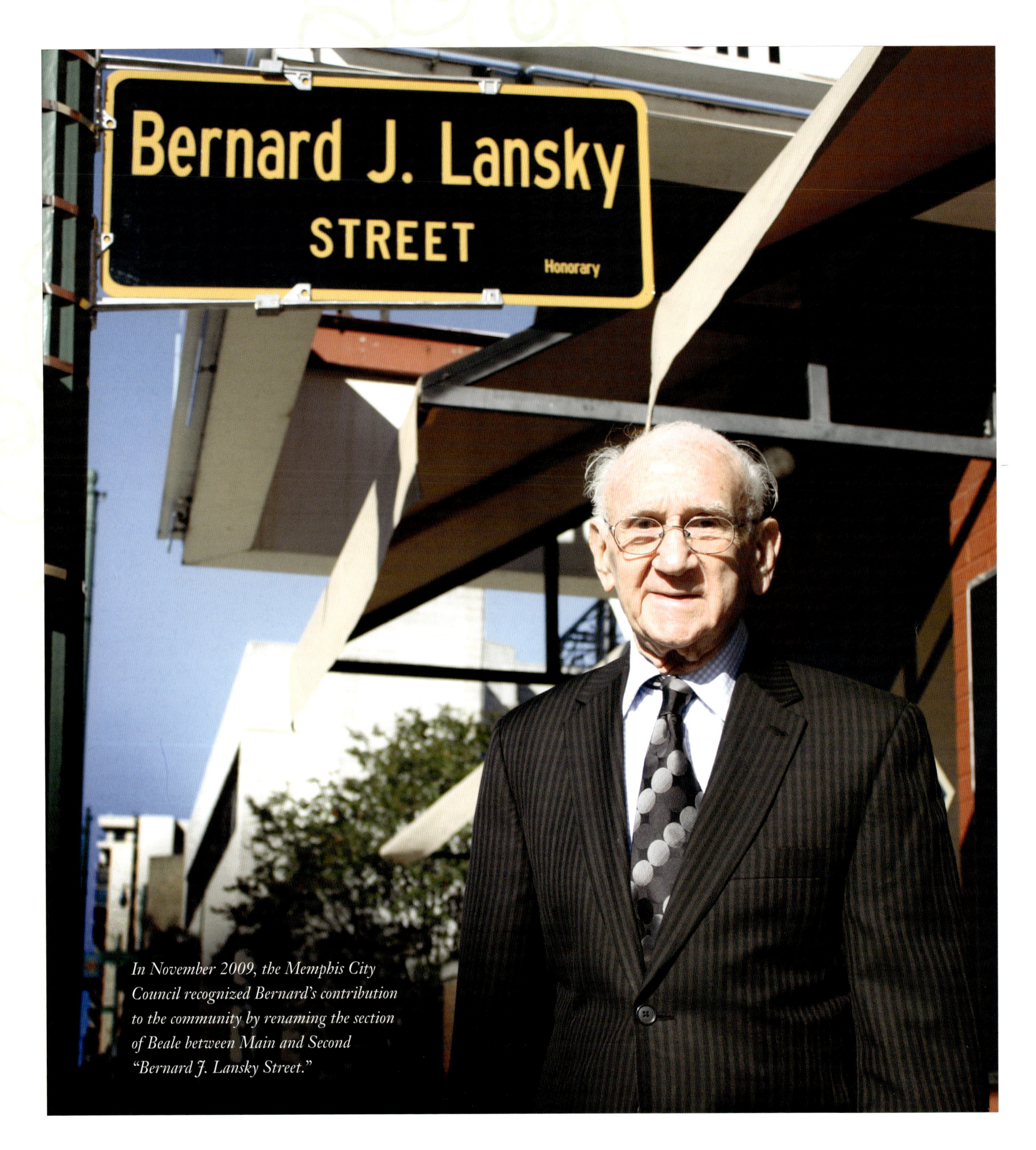

In November 2009, the Memphis City Council recognized Bernard's contribution to the community by renaming the section of Beale between Main and Second "Bernard J. Lansky Street."

ABOVE AND LEFT | **Duck and Cover**

Bernard receives his Peabody Duck Feet for the Peabody's Duck Walk Hall of Fame in 2006 from hotel owner Jack Belz. This award is given yearly to one outstanding individual who promotes downtown Memphis. Bernard's duck feet are located next to Elvis Presley's on Union Avenue, in front of the Lansky store.

THE LANSKY LEGACY 143

Lansky Brothers: Clothier to the King was designed, produced, and published by Beckon Books: 2451 Atrium Way, Nashville, Tennessee 37214. Beckon works with corporations, cultural attractions, and nonprofit organizations to identify, develop, and implement custom publishing programs. Beckon is located in San Diego, California and is an imprint of FRP, Inc. (Nashville, Tennessee). FRP is a member of the Southwestern/Great American family of companies.

Beckon Books is a trademark of FRP, Inc.
President: Christopher G. Capen
Design/Production: Monika Stout
Writer/Editor: Betsy Holt
www.beckonbooks.com
800-358-0560

Lansky Brothers
92 S Front Street
Memphis, TN 38103
901-525-5401
sales@lanskybros.com

Graceland/Elvis Presley Enterprises, Inc.
3734 Elvis Presley Boulevard
Memphis, TN 38116
901-332-3322

Copyright © 2010 Lansky Brothers of Memphis, Inc. All rights reserved. No part of this book may be reproduced or transmitted in any form or by any means, electronic or mechanical, including photocopying or recording, or by any information retrieval system, without the written permission of the copyright holder.

Lansky Brothers: Clothier to the King was published in cooperation with Elvis Presley Enterprises, Inc. Elvis and Elvis Presley are registered trademarks with the USPTO.

Lansky Brothers would like to thank the following people: Joyce Lansky and Geri Lansky, who could write their own book on being retailers' wives; Chris Capen, Monika Stout, Betsy Holt, and Sheila Thomas of Beckon Books for making this book happen; Carol Butler, Jack Soden, Robert Dye, Angie Marchese, and Erin Spurlock at Elvis Presley Enterprises; Jack, Marty, and Ron Belz of the Peabody hotel, where we have enjoyed nearly thirty years of business; our hard-working Lansky staff, who have dedicated themselves to making Lansky Brothers an international name; and finally, George Klein, David Porter, Jerry Schilling, Sam the Sham (Sam Samudio), and Robert Plant, our star customers who supplied quotations for us.

PHOTO CREDITS

Unless otherwise indicated, all images are property of the Bernard J. Lansky Collection.

Elvis photographs and artifact images used by permission, © Elvis Presley Enterprises, Inc. Elvis and Elvis Presley are registered trademarks with the USPTO.
Pages 40, 41A, 41B, 44, 46A, 47, 51A, 54C, 60A, 60B, 61B, 62A, 62B, 62C, 63, 70, 73C, 78B, 79A, 80A, 80B, 80C, 80D, 80E, 81, 84A, 85A, 85B, 85C, 86, 87A, 87B, 87C, 88A, 88B, 89A, 89B, 89C, 92-92, 94A, 95A, 95C, 96A, 96B, 96C, 98B

Photo by Robert W. Dye. Elvis image used by permission, Elvis Presley Enterprises, Inc.
Page 73

Photos © Alfred Wertheimer. All rights reserved.
Pages 52B, 53, 65, 68, 69, 104

Used by the permission of Peabody Management, Inc.
Pages 106, 120, 121A. 123A, 129

Photos courtesy of Steve Roberts
Pages 10-11, 12, 126, 130-131

Photos courtesy Memphis Archives
Pages 45A, 91A

Photo courtesy of the Don Newman Collection-Memphis Heritage
Page 23

CBS/Landov
Page 55

ISBN 978-1-935442-02-8

Library of Congress Catalog-in-Publication Data available through Beckon Books.

Printed in China
10 9 8 7 6 5 4 3 2 1
First Edition

WWW.LANSKYBROS.COM

LANSKY BROS.
126 BEALE AVE.
MEL ROSE
MANUFACTURING COMPANY
712 COMMERCE STREET DALLAS 2, TEXAS
APRIL 24TH., 1958
Stephen L. Stetson Co. LTD.
FINE HATS
LANSKY BROS
126 BEAL ST.
MEMPHIS, TENN.
ORDER NO 57
LEVI STRAUSS AND COMPANY
98 BATTERY STREET
SAN FRANCISCO 6, CALIFORNIA
STATEMENT
IN ACCOUNT WITH
Lansky Bros. Men's Shop
and Formal Rentals
UNITED STATES DEPOSITORY
PAY TO THE ORDER OF
Cash
Two hundred and 00/100
MEMPHIS, TENN.
DOLLARS
$200.00
Sire INC.
since 1850 makers of LEVI'S overalls
High Grade Shirts
SOLD TO
H 6862
78.00